I WANT TO BE ME

I WANT TO BE ME
It's Time to Put on Your TRUE Identity

Dr. Jim Bob Haggerton

©2025 All Rights Reserved. No portion of this book may be reproduced, stored in a retrieval system, or transmitted in any form or by any means—electronic, mechanical, photocopy, recording, scanning, or other—except for brief quotations in critical reviews or articles without the prior permission of the author.

Published by Game Changer Publishing

Paperback ISBN: 978-1-967424-56-6
Hardcover ISBN: 978-1-967424-57-3
Digital ISBN: 978-1-967424-58-0

www.GameChangerPublishing.com

DEDICATION

This book is dedicated to first and foremost, Jesus who saved me. To my wife Cindy—this story is half yours and without you I wouldn't be alive, much less here.

To my kids: Harper, Ellie, Evans, Tate, Whitten, Baker, and Crosby. You guys are my "why." You are why I am who I am and why I get to do what I do. Love you guys so much.

Lastly to Mrs. Stone, my high school English teacher. Thanks for teaching me to write, I hope this one gets an "A"!

I WANT TO BE ME

It's Time to Put on Your TRUE Identity

Dr. Jim Bob Haggerton

Table of Contents

Introduction 1

Chapter 1 – Admitting There's a Problem 5

Chapter 2 – Stuck 21

Chapter 3 – Overwhelm 37

Chapter 4 – Shame 49

Chapter 5 – Anxiety 61

Chapter 6 – Depression 75

Chapter 7 – Wanting to quit 89

Chapter 8 – Apathy 105

Chapter 9 – Bringing it All Together, Create Your Plan 119

Conclusion 131

Introduction

Hey there, I'm excited for you to read this book. I'm actually a little nervous because I'm pouring so much of who I am and the story of our family into this book. It really exposes all my flaws and all the things we walk through. So, who am I? I'm a dad, I'm a husband, I'm a business owner, a business coach, and an entrepreneur. The reason I'm able to pen this book and the way I got to where I am today is really just by walking out of the school of hard knocks. We walked out all of these stories as a family, and we have lived all the things that I'm gonna share with you in this book. They lead into the topics, steps, tips, and the things that I share with you in order to help you do one thing: GROW. In life, you can grow from experience and gain wisdom firsthand, *or* you can learn from someone else who has already done it. Trust me, learning from someone else is way less painful!

But besides the school of hard knocks, I had amazing mentors who came alongside me at different points in my journey, from sports team coaches to teachers, business coaches, partners, mentors, and pastors. They have just walked alongside my family, and held our hands. They have helped me along the way to become the leader and the husband and father that I am. I wrote this book as a guide to share what worked for me and our family and what may work for you from a mindset point of view or strategic standpoint. My prayer is that our stories and wisdom help inspire you to continue on the journey and to keep fighting, keep pushing, and keep walking when you want to give up. So, who is this book for? This book really is for anyone who wants to improve and thrive instead of just surviving. It's for you. It's for you if you are on the journey of improvement and if you're tired of being where you are when you know that there's better out there. If you're tired of just being the dad that you are right now, and you want to improve as a dad for your kids, if you want to improve in your communication with your wife, if you want to improve as a business owner, as a business leader, as an entrepreneur, as a steward of your finances, and all the different things that are around you; this book is for you.

And really, you should listen to me because I'm you. I've been right where you are. I've experienced everything I share. These are topics that I'm gonna bring up and talk to you about from a place of experience. I hope that when you read through the book, you feel hope. You are gonna get direction, but you're also gonna get practical steps at the end of each chapter because we've made this book into an interactive style guide for you to not only just read information but also get tips and training to help you strategically work through each category. There's also a community attached to this book. There are extra videos and training and teaching attached to each chapter to not only allow you to read the words on the page but also hear them, see them, and really be able to lead you through it. I hope you have clarity at the end of this book. You have clarity in where you are, where you need to be, what jersey you're currently wearing, and which one you really should be wearing. Thanks for trusting me to be your guide... see you on the other side.

CHAPTER 1

Admitting There's a Problem

Every jersey has a name on the back of it, a number, colors, and a team name. The purpose of a jersey is to identify you. It's to show *who* you are and to *what team* you belong. In sports, wearing the correct jersey is critical to your participation in that particular game. Jerseys give you identity. What would happen if you wore the wrong team's jersey onto the field? Or you wore a different player's jersey? Nothing positive! With that in mind, right off the bat, we have to figure out where we are. Because to get to where we want to go, we must figure out where we currently are.

Have you ever tried to take a trip and used your GPS (Google Maps or Waze for me)? It gives you two things to fill out before it shows you a map: Number one, the starting point, and number two, the destination.

Both are vital to map the best course for the journey you are taking. Life is no different. So where are you? This question can apply to your finances, your faith, your marriage, your health, or any other area you choose. Where are you? Some of you are probably stuck in a spot you shouldn't be, and there is an actual problem that we need to explore. Something is truly wrong or not going well. Maybe you just got diagnosed with something that is scaring you. Maybe you realize your marriage is falling apart. Perhaps you're figuring out how far in debt you are or how poorly your job or business is going. For others, you're just not where you want to be. Nothing is inherently wrong, but you just have not reached your potential or where you think you're called to. You're not in the job you're supposed to be in. You're not in the relationship you're supposed to be in. You're not as fit as you could be. Maybe you are happy in your marriage and with your kids, but you are positive it could be better.

We want to figure out where that is. But first, I need to take you back to a keynote speech I did and a vision the Lord gave me while I was speaking in Canton, Ohio, several years ago. I was at this church, giving a talk that actually centered on health and hormones. I remember it clearly: I was standing in this room, and I was getting ready to give a talk on health, and I looked up on this bulletin board, and there were all these different jerseys with different names on them, identifying different high school seniors. At that moment, I got this vision of people wearing jerseys every day. But what I saw was people wearing the wrong jerseys. I saw these people running out onto a field and playing football, but their jerseys were wrong! And I had this epiphany: What if the jerseys some of us are wearing aren't our jerseys? What if we were meant to wear a different jersey?

What if some of us are wearing titles on our backs of something or someone that's not us, and it is defining us and telling people who we think we are or have been told to be, but it's not a jersey that we're supposed to wear? Right there I changed my entire keynote and spoke on this instead! As I continued to flesh out this whole topic, I realized that the jerseys that we wear and the jerseys that some people put on us can relate to wounds, emotional issues, health issues, a life situation, or things we went through in our childhood. This is what we are going to explore in this book. We're going to talk about the jersey that you're currently wearing. And is that the jersey you should be wearing?

Is it the jersey that you chose to put on, or was this a jersey that someone put on you when you were a child? Was this a jersey that someone put over the top of your head and said, "This is who you're gonna be," or did they say, "This is who you are, this is who you're not," and you just believed it? For the rest of your life, you have been wearing this jersey, thinking that it defined who you were. Or did something happen to you along the way? Did something happen to your health? Did something happen in your life? Did something happen in your relationship? Did something scare you or hurt you, and it motivated you and pushed you out of where you were and caused you to put on a different jersey? We're going to talk about different jerseys that we normally see ourselves in and whether we're supposed to be.

Growing up, I remember putting on several jerseys. Some of those jerseys I wore really fit, and some didn't. I wore the jersey of ADOPTED, which fit me as a part of who I am because I was adopted as a baby. It's a true part of my story. But with ADOPTED came the wrong jerseys of REJECTED and UNWANTED. Some of these other jerseys were ones I put on myself and others ones that other people tried to put on me. Growing up, I constantly fought this mental battle of internally struggling with whether this jersey that said ADOPTED was a good thing or if I was going to believe what was written on the back of the other jerseys. Another jersey that people put on me was RESPONSIBLE; I felt constantly responsible for the people around me. I was responsible for my sister at the time, and I was put into situations and made to be more mature and act more mature than I really was. I constantly felt responsible for my friends or for certain situations, even from a young age, that I shouldn't have. A lot of that stemmed from my adoption story and that I wanted to constantly be needed and loved, and included. Those are things that I really had to wrestle with. Other jerseys were more natural and fit me well. TEAM CAPTAIN was an easy jersey for me to wear all through my teens. I truly knew who I was when it came to sports. I had an identity on those teams, and I knew my position exactly, and I knew exactly what I was supposed to do. In real life, though, it's different, and it's harder, and it's not as clear.

Sports give you a clear vision of who you are. When you put that jersey on, and you have your number, and you have a position, that jersey tells everyone in the stands what team you're on. It tells everybody in the stands who you are.

When you get into life, though, the jerseys are more subtle. When someone comes in, and you're trying to figure out who they are and they're wearing a jersey of ASHAMED or REJECTED, ABUSED, POWERFUL, or whatever it is, we're all trying to figure out what each other's jerseys are.

So we're going to explore that through this book, and we're going to figure out whether that jersey is what you're supposed to be wearing or not. I'm going to give you practical things to try and work through at the end of each chapter: I'll help you take off the wrong jersey that you are wearing now and find the right one. We're going to exchange it.

The first thing that we have to do is figure out where we are. Remember the GPS? On any kind of trip, if we don't know where we are and we're trying to figure out where we want to go, that GPS won't work. If I can't put in my GPS where I currently am, it has a really hard time telling me where I'm going and giving me a really good map in order to get there. It can't tell me how long it's going to take. It can't tell me any hazards along the way. It can't tell me possible stops along the way or anything that I may wanna see. I'm traveling blind! And so are you, without an understanding of where you are.

Finding where we currently are is key. And your current location doesn't always have to be a bad spot or a negative place. My wife, Cindy, and I are both super driven. We're entrepreneurs and run several businesses. Throughout the course of our marriage, we've constantly had this obsession and this mission of getting better. Personal development and growth have constantly been a value of ours, so we have pushed ourselves and put ourselves in situations to get better. We are constantly asking ourselves where we can improve not only in our businesses but also in our marriage, our parenting, and every realm we walk in. This is a value we are passing down to our kids as well. As a family, we are continually asking ourselves where we can improve or things the Lord wants us to change.

In many of these areas over the years, there weren't problems per se. There wasn't a major issue we needed to fix. We simply wanted to improve. We knew that the jerseys we were wearing weren't enough or weren't the final jersey we were meant to wear.

Many of you are in this place. You don't really find yourself in an emergency situation in your life. You feel like you're doing pretty great, actually, but you know there can be more.

Others reading this are in a different boat. Deciding where you are can be hard because of pride. Can you walk away from enough pride about what's going on in your life and lay that down, pick up humility, and choose to acknowledge that where you are right now isn't what it could be and decide to change?

For others reading this, you know you have an actual problem. There's something wrong. You know that it's not that it just could be better, but you took a wrong turn. You're not in the place that you need to be. You're not in the place that you're called to. You're not in the place that is bringing the best out of you, and you know you need to change. Maybe you made a major mistake. Perhaps you invested in the wrong deal. Or you were unfaithful in your marriage. Maybe you really messed up in your parenting. Whatever it is, you know it and feel it, and you know the jersey you are wearing is because of it. And you know it's time to change. But how do you do that?

To truly start the process of improvement, you have to acknowledge or admit where you are right now. OUCH! We can't minimize it or make excuses for it. At this point, you may have to admit to the problems you see. You may have to admit that there's a problem with your marriage. You're not acting like two teenagers in love anymore and are pretty much just roommates. You may need to admit that there's a problem in your parenting. You realize you yell at your kids all the time and aren't patient with them at all (hey, I'm preaching to myself here!) It may mean admitting that there's a problem in your finances. You made some bad decisions and haven't stewarded your finances well. I've been there multiple times. Or perhaps you need to admit that there is a problem in your business, time management, communication skills, or in your diet. Whatever it is for you, you have to accept that there's a problem and acknowledge it.

This isn't a quick or easy process. PHEW! If someone tells you they don't struggle with this step, then they are lying to you. So don't beat yourself up, and don't rush this. You'll see me talk about counseling and community a lot in this book, and this is probably a great spot to get someone to help you walk this out. Another pro tip: If you journal, this would be a good time to pull it back out. If you're not, this might be a great time to start!

When you drill down deep and find that one area you really need to work on, you'll know. You'll feel it in your gut, and if you're like me, you may want to puke. That's because there are so many emotions tied to who you are, even if who you thought you were all these years was wrong, and setting a path to change is *a lot* for your brain to process.

Let yourself go through the emotions of what that means to be able to make a choice to move in a new direction and to make better choices for the future. I will talk more about this and give you practical steps to work yourself through the process of change.

Cindy and I often have to work through this as parents. We have seven kids total (some of you just fainted). Six kids are here on earth. We parent our sixth kid, Crosby, differently than we did our oldest son, Harper. We have learned things as we've gone through parenting, and we've had to take a hard look and go, "Ooh, that thing that we did there, that way that we communicated, that way that we disciplined, that way that we talked to him or our choices with his diet, that wasn't the best choice for him" (sorry bud). And we've had to pivot. We've had to admit we could have done better in seasons, so we've constantly gotten better over time. (Even though we still feel like failures as parents and never feel like we've made it! Anyone else? No, just me? Okay.) If we had never looked at our parenting, sought mentors, and taken the time to question our tactics and strategy, we would never have adapted and would have never made better choices. This same process applies to every area of your life.

Why am I telling you that? Because I love to admit that our oldest has needed counseling because of us. Of course not! I want you to understand that we are no better than anybody else in this book; I'm just further along the journey than some of you. And even if you are further along the journey than I am, maybe you can identify and see yourself in my story. Throughout this book, I want to share stories and share what we're doing, what we've done, and what we've walked through to be able to figure out the jerseys that we're wearing in our own family, figure out the issues that we processed and grew through, figure out where we are in the transition of our journeys and in this GPS called life, what we've done to break out of it, and what we've done to move ahead. All of this comes back to mindset.

> *"Do not conform to the pattern of this world, but be transformed by the renewing of your mind. Then you will be able to test and approve what God's will is—his good, pleasing and perfect will."*
> – (Romans 12:2)

The first thing that we should do is figure out where our mind is because everything in our body and everything in our choices starts with a thought. Romans 12:2 says that the way we are to be transformed is by the renewal of our minds. It doesn't say to be transformed by the renewal of your diet or to be transformed by the renewal of your adrenal glands or your liver (weird, I know). It talks about your mind because everything flows out of thoughts. Your thoughts turn into actions, and your actions turn into habits. It's how you think about the things that you're doing, how you parent, how you manage your finances, how you eat, or any of the things that you're walking out that determine the choices that you're going to make. And the choices that you make over time determine the habits and systems that you build (good or bad), and those habits end up becoming who you are. We have to start by looking at our mindset. You have to really ask yourself, *Do I have a poverty mindset?* Or *Do I have a growth mindset?*

A poverty mindset is when someone looks at everything and only sees what they don't have or sees the downside of every single possible situation and only the negative that could happen. This is different from someone who is more pessimistic in personality. Some people naturally see the issues or problems with choices or situations (and thank God for that!), and it helps them plan, but they don't only see the negative, and they don't dwell on it.

Like I just said above, this isn't a personality-driven issue. This literally is a mindset. It is a choice and is where someone is choosing to set their thoughts and focus. Personalities that are less positive by nature may have to work harder to see the positive and the good, but negativity doesn't have to be their identity or main focus.

A poverty mindset looks at everything and immediately knows it's not gonna work (ever known anyone like that; your mother-in-law, maybe?) They immediately go to the side of negativity and never look at or consider other possibilities. In any category in your life, if you allow yourself to have a poverty mindset, you automatically assume the worst and assume you will fail. You assume the new business venture will fail before you start. You assume and expect your new job position to be terrible or your new boss to be the worst. You assume your new wife or husband doesn't appreciate you or will cheat on you. You assume that the diet won't work for you or the fitness plan will fail. (Bring on the Blue Bell ice cream!) As a parent with poverty mentality, you *never* look at the fact that you were born to do this. That you were chosen to parent these kids. That you were chosen to be in this marriage. You were chosen to run this business. You immediately see the negative and don't want to grow in it. Is this stepping on your toes yet? If not, I'll step harder! Don't feel bad; we all fall into this category at one time or another. I'm a naturally super positive person, but I find myself slipping into this at different times. It can happen to any of us. It can happen when we are exhausted or mad. It can come out of trauma or being hurt, and emotionally, we don't want to deal with what's in front of us, so we shut down. The important part is acknowledging it so that we can change it.

So, what does it look like if we operate out of a growth mindset? Someone who has a growth mindset is constantly looking for ways to improve. They constantly see issues or situations, they see problems, or maybe they see where they are, and instead of getting stuck in the mud of all of the bad that could happen, or all of the negativity, or all of the bad situations or the bad outcomes, they choose to focus on possibilities. They choose to focus on solutions, and they choose to focus on creating a plan in order to move forward. Now, I know some of you are sitting there thinking, *Well, that sounds great. If I were like that, I would just lie to myself and pretend everything is great!* My wife Cindy says this to me sometimes. However, having a growth mindset isn't about not acknowledging the issues in front of you; it's choosing not to let the problem defeat you but focusing on solutions. Let's go back to the GPS analogy I used earlier. If you have a poverty mentality, and the GPS says that there's a detour up ahead, you will get frustrated and think, *Ugh! I have to take a detour, so I'm not gonna go any further on this. I'm done.* And you wanna give up on the trip that you're on. You will abandon ship without looking at any other options or possibilities. I'm going to say this a hundred times throughout this book, but this is why who you surround yourself with is so important.

A poverty mentality or mindset tries to shut you down and stop you, whereas a growth mindset and mentality says, *Hey, this is just a detour. That means I'm going to get back on the same path. I just need to figure out where to go. I need to slow down to figure out what we need to do next.* I've gone through different stages in my own life of poverty versus growth mentality. And what you're going to find is that in different seasons of your life, you'll battle or have to work through a poverty mindset over and over and over again. At some point, you will sit there and work through a poverty mindset in your marriage. And you will think, *Man, I've got this! I've arrived, we're good!* And then you get six months to a year down the road, and something else happens, and BOOM, it comes right back up again. And you know what? That's okay. This is a lifelong journey. And that's a key thing to think about: This journey is fluid, and we're on it for the rest of our lives. We are constantly growing, changing, and adjusting, and we have to choose to dig in and remember that this is a battle. This is a spiritual battle we are in. There's an enemy who wants you to fail and will try every tactic to try to force you to give up and quit. We have to keep filling ourselves with the truth of scripture and the support of people around us to stay in the fight and continue to improve.

When I graduated from chiropractic college and went into private practice, I thought I had a growth mindset and that I was ready. I'd worked on myself for several years and had made it. I was super excited, but I was so naïve.

I was young, passionate, and idealistic, and then I got out into practice, and I figured out that it was a lot harder and lonelier out there on my own trying to build a practice, trying to market the practice, and trying to bring patients into the office while paying bills, paying overheads, and paying for equipment and everything else.

I found myself getting pulled into a poverty mindset. I started feeling sorry for myself. I started making excuses and blaming people around me: my patients, my staff, insurance companies, or my landlord. I began to fall into this victim trap. It felt like this was always gonna be this way, and it was never going to change. I found myself slipping, and I had to find my way back out. And I did. Over the 15 years I was in full-time private practice, that wasn't the only time I had to fight through negativity or feeling hopeless. It would come up at different times, and with the help of the people in my corner, we would rise up and find a way. I'll help you figure out how in each chapter that follows.

In this book, I'm going to use different analogies and stories from our family because we've walked out many hard things. We've walked through a lot of seasons in our lives, and each one has offered us an opportunity to learn and grow. Each different season in our family has been an opportunity for us to stop and ask, "What are we supposed to learn from this? Where is this going to take us next?"

You get the choice when these questions come up to use them as springboards or as walls or barriers. In the next few chapters, I will cover the types of mindsets that will try to stop you. These include the jerseys that you wear that are incorrect and the jerseys that you start to label yourself with that start to change your mindset from being growth-oriented and start to push you into having a poverty mindset.

I'm going to use different stories of things our family has gone through, and hopefully, that will resonate with you. Hopefully, you will see yourself in some of those and also see that what you are walking through is not hopeless. The different places that you find yourself in right now are not hopeless. If we ever get to the point where we lose hope, then we have a real problem. But as long as we keep hope in each situation and know that there is hope, no matter what, we can get out of any situation and into a better place. No matter how hopeless your marriage feels or how it feels with your finances, when you understand there is always hope, then you can make real change. What it really comes down to are these questions. Who can help you out of that spot and walk with you? And what are practical steps to take each day, one step at a time, to keep moving forward?

"I have told you these things, so that in me you may have peace.
In this world you will have trouble. But take heart!
I have overcome the world."
– (John 16:33).

Scripture promises us that we will have problems. The last part of that verse says to "take heart" because Jesus has already overcome the world. When you know that there's hope, you know that all you have to do is put one foot in front of the other, take one day at a time, one morning at a time, one minute at a time, and keep moving forward. You can get yourself out of any single situation because you're going to look back at where you are now and where you are in a month from now, and where you are a year from now will be completely different. All because you just put one foot in front of the other.

I need to ask you to do something for me as you read this book. I need you to be open-minded. I want you to lay down your pride and literally go, "Hey, you know what? I know that I can be better." And I want you to be able to open your mind, release any preconceived notions you have about what you have tried before, and just jump into all this with me. Choose to dive into this with me. Dive into the stories, dive into the concepts, and think about the jerseys that you wear on a daily basis. Think about whether that really defines you, and then decide if that's the jersey that you want to wear or if you need to make an exchange. You can do this, and I'm here to help. Let's get started.

To access our free BONUS course on Mindset Change and Community

SCAN THE QR CODE:

CHAPTER 2

Stuck

As an adopted child, I grew up on a working farm and ranch in West Texas near Midland. We farmed cotton and wheat and raised cattle. Honestly, it was a perfect childhood growing up in the middle of nowhere. One of the things that we did when we were plowing cotton was what we call sand fighting. We had tons of sand storms out there (think *Twister*, but with dirt), and our livelihood in farming depended on us keeping these crops alive long enough for us to be able to harvest. When the wind got up, it would blow all the loose sand on the top of the ground, and at those speeds, if we couldn't stop it, it would burn the young cotton plants and ruin an entire crop. The sand fighter plows had a whole row of wheels with little scoops on them to dig a few inches into the ground to get to the wetter, more stable soil and calm down the loose sand. They would help to keep everything from blowing away while not injuring the young cotton plants. When this happened, though, it was fast, furious, and stressful!

In West Texas, it rarely rained. When it did, it flooded, and it was borderline dangerous. There were times when we had enough rain, though, and it created wet spots in the low spots out in the middle of the field that were really hard to see. But when we needed to go out and sand fight, it didn't matter. We had to get out in the middle of it because if we didn't get out as soon as the sandstorm hit, it could burn up the whole crop, and we'd lose everything. When I was around 10 or 12, I was driving a big tractor into a field. My dad was plowing another field over a half mile away from me. A huge sandstorm was coming, and we were rushing to get the crop protected. There was always pandemonium when a sandstorm came up on the horizon. We dropped everything, ran to get these sand fighters, and rushed off. I flew out into the middle of this field with a tractor that was not four-wheel-drive when I hit a low spot in the middle of the field. There was so much mud, and it was so deep that my front two wheels stopped turning, and I buried the tractor in the mud. Instead of getting off and waiting or running to get one of my cousins or go get my uncle or my dad, I tried as hard as I could to get the tractor out of the mud. I went forward and backward and forward and backward until I had that tractor up to the axles in mud! I was scared of what my dad would say when he figured out I had got the tractor stuck on top of messing up the field (he hated that), creating these huge ruts and holes, and tearing up part of his crop. It was a bad day.

So I got out, trembling and scared, and walked down to the next field to find my dad. We went back over to try to pull it out of the mud but decided we had to leave it and pull it out another day. I was cooked, as my teens would say. Fear had gotten me stuck.

I learned a lot from that experience. When you're in a spot that you know you've got to get out of, you have a couple of choices. When you are stuck, sometimes you can power your way through. You can figure it out, and you can bear down, roll up your sleeves, rely on your wit and your grit, and get yourself out. Sometimes that's possible. There are times you know you need to push a little harder. You know you need to dig in and not give up. Other times, you need to admit you're stuck and acknowledge that the actions and effort that got you where you are won't be the same ones to get you out.

The only way we got that tractor unstuck was to wait a few days for the ground to dry out. It took a while, and my dad was not happy. Then, we had to bring in a bigger tractor that had four-wheel drive, hook it up, and pull the rig out. Hmmm, this sounds like a life lesson. I had to go get another piece of equipment that was more experienced and better suited for the job and get the help to pull that tractor out. In life, we sometimes have to do the exact same thing, don't we? We have to stop doing the same old thing and stop creating ruts. And we have to stop and admit that we're stuck. We're stuck in that certain spot in your marriage where you don't want to be, and you're not happy. Or you're stuck in business, and nothing you try works, and you don't feel like there's any solution or way out. But like the good go-getter you are, you're going to just keep spinning your wheels as much as you can, trying to dig yourself out. And you need to just stop. And you need to go find somebody to ask for help to pull you out.

That again goes back to Chapter 1 and just admitting to yourself there is a problem: *Hey, I am stuck. I have tried all I can and done all I can at this moment on my own, and I need help.* The beautiful thing about asking for help from someone who has been where you are is they have the wisdom to help you see the solutions and see the end from the beginning. But this is hard because it takes so much humility to do so. But if we do this in so many situations, it would keep us from making an even bigger mess. It would keep us from making more of a rut and getting more stuck in that same area.

So what is it that keeps us constantly digging in the same hole and stuck in the same ruts and getting us more and more stuck? What is that thing? I really believe it boils down to fear. Fear of someone finding out that we don't know as much as we think we do. Fear of us being exposed as not being as great as we thought we were. Fear of having to ask for help, fear of letting people down, or fear of failing at anything and everything. That was my fear growing up: fear of failing.

Growing up adopted, I had this fear of not being loved, of being rejected, or abandoned. I was terrified of failing because I felt I earned my acceptance and my place in my own family, with my friends, my teammates, and everyone else, by achieving and succeeding at things. Admitting I failed was the worst-case scenario. That was the endgame for me all those years. I would rather create such a rut and get so stuck and create so many problems for myself and everybody else than fail.

You could tell where that tractor had gotten stuck for the next two or three cycles we planted crops. It messed up the ground so badly that there was evidence of it for years. If I had stopped sooner and gone for help sooner, the long-term damage would have never happened. But it was fear that kept me from doing that, getting help, and from stopping the tractor, and that's exactly what ended up happening in my marriage.

We were successful in our practice, and things were moving so fast. I should have pumped the brakes, but I didn't. There was fear and pride that kept me from slowing down in 2011 when I really felt like it was out of control and I felt unseen. I didn't feel like Cindy and I were in a good place. I didn't know what it was. I didn't know how to put my finger on it. I just knew I felt like we were two ships drifting further and further apart.

But instead of asking for help, instead of being super upfront and honest about it, instead of going and getting help, I created a rut. I got myself stuck in a bad place inside our marriage, and I had an extramarital affair with my wife's best friend. I had never been or felt more stuck in my life.

You may have felt this way before, too. Some of you feel like, "I am stuck in this one thing, this job that I've been in for so many years, and running through a bunch of ruts making it worse. I don't know how to change it." Others of you may feel stuck as I did in 2011 and 2012. Stuck in these choices that you made, knowing that if I had asked for help or we had got any kind of counsel, things could have been different. I wouldn't have kept burying my marriage so deep that it would take a miracle to pull out.

The affair lasted about a year; I turned around in 2012 and knew I was stuck in a bad place. But I didn't know how to get out of it. I didn't know how I was going to get out of that situation. I thought my marriage was over. I thought my practice was over. I thought I would lose everything else, too, like my friends and children. I thought that everything was about to fall down around me.

In situations like I found myself, you have two choices. You can either just put it in park, or you can put your whole life in neutral, wait for a second, admit that life is not going in a good direction or where you wanted it to, and ask for help. Hit your knees and ask the Lord for help, get professional help and counsel, and discuss matters with a financial professional or a coach to be able to look at your business and ask you some hard questions. It's really hard to know what questions to ask and what direction to go when it seems so dark and hopeless. And if this has been building up for a while.

Do you know that even the financial situation that you're in right now is a compilation of the choices you made three to five years ago? The thousands of choices made over that period all culminated in where you are right now. Success or trouble doesn't happen overnight. There's a journey and a process that puts you in the position you are to either win or struggle. It takes time to get there, but it takes time to get out.

Asking questions to gain a new perspective and a new mindset is gonna position you differently. A new mindset leads to new choices and new habits. New habits lead to a completely different life. And that's the same in any different category in your life. That's the same in marriage, finances, and parenting—things don't change immediately. Things don't turn around and look differently immediately. We have to make different choices, and that starts with a different mindset. Then, making the right choices for a consistent period puts us in a new location.

I got out of the affair, and the Lord healed our marriage in 2012. Through lots of counseling, tears, and late nights, we made it. The next year, 2013, we were feeling amazing about how far we'd come in restoring our marriage. We found out that we were pregnant with our third baby, and we were literally elated and felt so blessed that we were in that situation. We felt like it was redemption for all the pain and mess. We seriously thought all our trials and tests and hard times were behind us. Our business was booming again, Cindy was thriving and the pregnancy was going well, our kids were happy, and we were back on top of the world. We had no idea what was coming.

On June 14, 2014, Cindy went in for an emergency delivery. She hadn't been feeling good that week, and we'd chalked it up to stress and anxiety. I flew out of town the day before to help my mom with my dad in Santa Fe, New Mexico. But after a conversation with her on the phone that morning, I knew something was wrong. I called our midwife to take her to the hospital, and I rushed to the airport to get a flight. We found out that Evans, our son, had some genetic abnormalities, and she went into early labor at 33 weeks and ended up delivering him that day while I was on my flight. He lived only two hours.

Evans was diagnosed with Potter's Syndrome, had underdeveloped lungs and kidneys, and couldn't sustain normal life in the real world. We went from everything being so good, healing, and doing amazing to rock bottom again, all in just a few hours. We left that hospital with an empty car and no baby. That was seriously one of the longest 20-minute car rides of my entire life. All the wind had been knocked out of me. It felt like trying to breathe with a wet blanket over your face.

Our other two children were staying with friends overnight, so we went back to the house. We felt stuck again. It was a horrible mixture of grief, sorrow, rage, and fear. It was paralyzing.

The affair was horrible, but it was nothing compared to this. This felt hopeless and dark. It felt like if I tried to do anything at all, if I moved at all, if I did anything, if I made any decisions, I was going to make it worse. And so, out of fear, I just sat there in my stuckness. I knew I would stay stuck. And I was going to sit here as stuck as I was because I didn't want it to get any worse.

One of the most important things that helped Cindy and me out of our immediate paralysis and shock was our friends. They were waiting for us when we pulled into the driveway at our house at 2:00 a.m. They cried with us, let us yell at them, and were always close by, and a phone call or text away over the next few weeks and months because they had gone through this journey themselves. They had lost a son themselves a couple of years before, and they understood what we would go through. They had a different perspective because they were further along on their grief journey. They didn't allow us to stay stuck in our fear and grief, but they didn't rush us either. They also didn't allow us to fall into two of the other traps that we can step into in harder times of our lives: complacency or laziness.

As a child, if I had a day off and I was caught lying around or had nothing to do, my dad told me that I was being lazy. And so I filled my days with all kinds of stuff. Believe me, I had to heal over that later. (You should just start a counseling fund for your kids now.) I had to work on not being a workaholic and not being obsessed with work later on, but as a kid and teen growing up, laziness or doing nothing was not acceptable. Laziness can be a factor where you just don't wanna do things, and because you don't wanna do things, then nothing changes. This can be a response to trauma, like after we lost our son, or it can be a product of and the fruit of your bad habits. I know one of my favorite quotes is, "Nothing changes if nothing changes." So if we don't change anything, then nothing will ever change in our lives. Laziness can be the shackle that keeps you in a bad place for too long.

Complacency is similar to laziness, but instead of having no desire to do anything, complacency is just not caring. Complacency is when I'm in a situation that is negative, but I don't really care, and I don't really see the severity or the importance of the choices that I'm making because I *choose* not to see them. This is a slight difference, but it's a big one. It's about not bothering to put any effort into something or not really worrying about making better choices. It's really not having a vision for your situation and how everything works together. I'm convinced that if we really saw how everything worked together and was linked from beginning to end, we would have a higher chance of making better choices.

The days that we waste being complacent or the days that we waste being lazy or not moving ahead, we never get those back. I had a professor when I attended a seminary at our local church. I went to ministry school for two years, and one of our professors had what he called his *Akarit* message. It is a Hebrew word and a Jewish message that he said is really not translatable into English, but the whole point of it was knowing the end from the beginning. He said that if we knew the end from the beginning, then we would make different decisions earlier on and not have to experience the same suffering. This relates to the things we have control of. Now, obviously, losing our son wasn't something we could control. That's why it's just so important to always be prepared and be ready in any scenario, and it matters who's around you.

When we said goodbye to Evans, the nurses were who I really remember clearly. How compassionate they were and how patient they were with us as we processed what was happening and as we helped our kids process. I also remember the family and friends that were in that room and that surrounded that bed and loved us. They prayed over us, cried with us, and held us as we said goodbye to him with Harper and Ellie. That group of people carried us through that experience and would continue to carry us through over the next few days, weeks, and months. Those people were one of the biggest reasons we did not stay stuck in that season.

If you're going to fight getting stuck all your life, it's the people around you who will make sure that you don't stay stuck. You have to make that mental choice. Again, it always goes back to our mindset. Once we get stuck, we have to make the decision not to stay there, right? (Pouting only works so long!) And much of that comes back to knowing that it is worth us getting unstuck. People need you out there. The world needs you. Your family, your wife, your kids, your business, your friends, your church, and your community need you. The world needs you out there, being the best version of you that you can be, living out your purpose. And they're not going to get that if you stay stuck.

So, have the mindset and make the choice never to let yourself stay stuck. Are you going to get stuck sometimes? Sure. Was that time on the tractor the only time that I ever got stuck with equipment on the ranch? Of course not. I got lots of machinery stuck. I got four-wheelers stuck. I got pickup trucks stuck. I got all kinds of things stuck, but we never left them that way. We never left it and didn't go fix the situation and get unstuck. Hopefully, that rings a bell and makes sense.

When you go through different situations and feel stuck, the biggest thing that helps you is having a purpose in everything that you do. Jon Acuff is one of my favorite authors, and in one of his books, *Start*, he writes that people are always looking for a purpose in their lives. They're always asking, "What's my purpose? What am I here for?" He says we need to stop looking for purpose and just live with purpose every single day. BOOM! I love that! Just LIVE with purpose because once you have a purpose, all the other things that happen, whether it's the loss of a child, the loss of a business, debt, an injury, or something that comes up, you're not only able to make it through successfully, you are able to help others around you. Want to get unstuck? Having a purpose that will help other people find hope and healing will get you unstuck. That's like a tractor that hooks onto you and pulls you out of the mud to help you keep going. It's something to latch on to and to grab hold of in order to get you out of where you currently are. And that's important. So, find the purpose in every single thing you're doing. Find a purpose in your marriage so that when you get stuck, you reach out, and you can pull yourself out of it. You can pull your marriage along.

We recently were at a business retreat in Colorado Springs, where they had a breakout session on marriage. The speakers were missionaries in Latin America and had been through hard and difficult experiences. The main thing they spoke about was the importance of having a clear purpose in your marriage and what you are working together for. They talked about being on the same page with our purpose and that all the little things that get in the way and cause fights and issues aren't that big of a deal because they don't change the purpose. The clear, common purpose keeps you focused on where you are going together so that you don't get caught up in the common traps of the enemy.

Find the purpose in your parenting. Know the purpose and what you're going for. Know what you're shooting for. Know your goal. That way, you can pull yourself out of those days that just feel like an eternity when all the kids are fighting and nothing's going right, and you feel like it's a waste of time. Remember, you're never losing if you're learning. If you went through situations and lost—we lost our son after the Lord had brought us through the affair and financial hardship—we've always turned around and said, "Man, what do we need to learn from this?" If you don't learn from history, it's bound to repeat itself.

If we don't learn from the things that we live through, then we're going to repeat them because we don't understand what got us in that situation in the first place. If I didn't learn from the time I got that tractor stuck and I had to walk miles to find my dad—if I didn't learn when the field looks like this or when I'm running a sand fighter, I need to look for these key things to make sure that there's not a lot of mud around —if I didn't learn from that, I would have done it again, but I never got another tractor stuck in the mud like that.

So, what jersey exchange do you need to make? If you're wearing a jersey that says STUCK, try exchanging it for one that says FREE or OPEN because you're open-minded, open to change, and open to finding the purpose in the area since you know there's a reason for everything that happens. You have to believe that. You have to understand that the Lord doesn't make mistakes.

> *"And we know that in all things, God works for the good of those who love him, who have been called according to his purpose."*
> *– (Romans 8:28)*

God did not and does not make mistakes with you. He does not make mistakes about where He has you. And He does not put you in situations to punish you because He's mean or He's mad at you or something. He puts you in situations and leaves you there because He loves you, and He's got a purpose and a plan for your life. So, if you know that He's got a purpose and a plan for your life, and you know that there's a reason why you're here, and you know there's a reason you are experiencing any of the situations you are, then you can be open and expectant about where He's going to take you. So take that jersey and switch it out today.

Nerd Depot: The Science

So, what happens in the science of your mind when you get stuck? What happens to your hormones? Our body and our neurology must process every single thing that we experience. It has to understand what's happening and make sense of everything it's experiencing every single millisecond. The primary goal is to keep you safe.

Often, over the past 21 years of helping thousands of patients, I found many who felt really sick or injured were just deficient in something they needed or had a simple toxicity. So, if you can put back in the missing thing or remove the thing not needed, the body can heal. Things like this that affect the function of the body can make events you go through feel worse than they actually are. It's hard enough to grow and deal with stress and change when your body is functioning at 100 percent. But when it's not, that's a whole different thing altogether.

Some of the biggest factors that feed the feeling of being stuck are exhaustion, lack of sleep, lack of protein, too much screen time, or not enough consistency in the diet.

1. **Exhaustion.** Lack of sleep or rest. Your brain and neurotransmitters (signals in the brain) thrive and function at their best with adequate sleep and rest. Without that, you are running on fumes, and your body cannot process life at the speed that it happens. Lack of sleep in and of itself leads to anxiety, depression, and extra cortisol problems in the endocrine system. I could write an entire book just on this and on not taking a rest day, but let's go to another factor.

2. **Lack of protein.** In order to heal and repair tissue in your body that gets consistently damaged every day due to stress and daily activity, you have to have enough protein. If you don't, your body will break down slowly. Plus, the only way to have enough nutrition to make sound decisions is to ensure you have enough quality protein in your diet. Protein is the building block of your neurotransmitters. A gram of protein for every pound of body weight is a good starting point. Quality matters here, as with everything in your diet, so make sure you are getting high-quality protein.

3. **Excess screen time.** Phones, iPads (like the one I used to write this book), and TVs. We love the technology we have to get life done and get ahead as a species, but they very well may be the things that destroy us. Not counting the ways that screens cause imbalance in our neurology, the effects of blue light alone are enough to motivate us to spend less time on them. Being on screens late at night will also negatively affect the sleep we so desperately need. Try to limit them as much as possible, especially at the end of the day, and even when not, try using blue light-blocking glasses.

4. **Diet inconsistency.** This points to blood sugar irregularity. If we aren't consistent in getting proper nutrition, our blood sugar will not stay stable, and this will affect not only our mood and ability to think clearly, but our stress levels and our body's ability to handle that stress. Eating at a similar time helps to keep our blood sugar regulated.

All of those things can and will cause problems with your body feeling stuck, feeling complacent, or like you just don't want to make a choice. You need the right amount of nutrition to make your brain and body work. So be consistent and make the changes, and you'll be shocked by how your body responds.

We have built out a custom questionnaire for you to evaluate how stuck you may think you are and what to do. To access this and the community,

SCAN THE QR CODE:

CHAPTER 3

Overwhelm

I don't know about you, but there have been multiple times in my life (and many more to come, I'm sure) where I've just felt overwhelmed to the point where I'm almost frozen. My brain asks, *What do I do?* I really just freeze. You've heard of fight, flight, or freeze? It's the response your body has to stressors. In the *freeze* spot of that stress response, your body just gets overwhelmed, your brain is overwhelmed, you have no idea what to do, and to not make something worse, you do nothing, and you sit there and just freeze. Anybody else ever feel that way?

I was interviewing a good friend who is an amazing entrepreneur. She said, "I never use the word 'overwhelmed.' Every time I feel overwhelmed, I stop, and I go, 'Thank you, God, for believing in me so much that you would bring all of this to me, even though I don't feel like I can handle it.'" I just thought, *WWWHHHUUUUTTTTT?*

She continued, "And then I sit there and pray, Lord, make me into the person I'm supposed to be to handle all these things that you've brought me."

That rocked me and convicted me so much. I had to stop and take it in. I'm a really positive person and usually a really grateful person, but I had been overwhelmed with our kids, our schedule, and our multiple businesses. And it really made me reflect, reset, and rethink my responses when I felt overwhelmed. I needed to be thankful and say, "Lord, thank you for all of this. Who do I need to become in order to handle these things?" I think it's the same for all of us. Who do you need to become when you are overwhelmed?

The week before Evans passed, we were living in my in-laws' house. We had two small kids and were getting our house ready to sell. A couple of days before, my mom called in a panic. My parents were going from their home in Colorado to Texas, and on the way, my dad got a really severe kidney infection, and they had to stop at the hospital in Santa Fe, New Mexico. They were scared and concerned and really wanted me to come out there to help her. Cindy hadn't been feeling good. She was 33 weeks pregnant, and I didn't want to leave her at home, but we discussed it, and she told me she really felt like I needed to be there, so I booked a flight.

I flew to Santa Fe to meet my parents. Dad was really sick, and I stayed with him for a few days, but I had a bad feeling about Cindy and the pregnancy. It was like this deep dread and anxiety. I couldn't shake it. I didn't want to bug Cindy, so I didn't say anything that day and focused on my dad, who had turned septic at this point and needed some pretty high-powered antibiotics to make sure he didn't get worse.

On Saturday morning in Santa Fe, we went to check on my dad. I called Cindy to talk to her and to check how she was feeling, and something just did not feel right. I felt alarmed. I felt this fear over me. She assured me she was fine, but I knew she was lying and trying to make me feel okay about it since I was out of town.

So, I called our midwife who was watching a movie with her husband. When I told her, "I think something's wrong, and I want you to go check the baby and make sure that Cindy's okay," they immediately did as I asked.

Later, the midwife called and said, "You need to find a flight home. Cindy is going into labor. She's already dilated. We're rushing her to the hospital. You need to get home as fast as possible." I was overwhelmed, and I froze. I sat there and didn't know what to do. I was in a hospital room in Santa Fe, and my dad was in bed with an IV. When I got off the phone, I told my mom and sat there looking shocked because I didn't know what to do. My mom is amazing in emergencies and she didn't disappoint in this one. She jumped up and said, "Come on, let's go! We have to run!" She grabbed me, pulled me out of the chair and took off running down the hallway of the hospital to get to the car to rush to the hotel to get my stuff. Then we drove as fast as possible to the airport. We were like Ace Ventura screeching in on two wheels. I'm positive my mom thought we would die that day.

There was a single flight left back to Dallas, and we had less than an hour. I ran up to the counter right as the attendant was putting a counter closed sign up because they were leaving to finish loading the plane. I put on every ounce of southern charm I had in my body and begged, "Hello, ma'am, I've gotta get back to Dallas. My wife is pregnant and has gone into early labor."

She smiled, opened her computer back up, and said, "Well, it's your lucky day. There's one seat left." ONE seat left on the plane? If you don't believe that God has a plan for things, you're completely wrong. There was a single seat left. She got me on the plane that was leaving in less than 15 minutes.

I still felt so overwhelmed because there was nothing I could do from a whole state away. I was in New Mexico. Cindy was in Texas. She was at the hospital with our birth team and friends taking care of her, but she was about to have our baby there without me. I was terrified.

While in the air, I received a text that came through randomly—I guess we flew through a pocket of cell phone connection. It was from our midwife, and she said, "Baby here, it's a boy. Hurry, it's not good." There was no more reception and no more texts. That was IT. I sat there shaking and thinking, *What exactly does that mean?* That's when I panicked. I was in the front row of the plane and didn't know what to do. I began to pray frantically. And softly, I heard two simple words, "Worship me." I was still shaking, but a feeling of peace rushed over me, so I started playing worship music on my headphones.

The music calmed me down until I landed in Dallas, where a friend picked me up. This also bothered me because it was supposed to be my father-in-law coming to get me. I knew something wasn't right. At the hospital, I rushed up to the room to see Cindy. The minute I got there, she literally said, "Jim Bob, he's not going to make it." I was crushed. I'd come all that way. I'd prayed my eyes out. I'd cried my eyes out. I'd got all the way to the hospital room, thinking, *Man, this is going to be it. Our miracle. We're going to figure this out. The Lord's going to heal him. We're going to have an option for this. We're going to have a solution.* Instead, Cindy said that Evans wasn't going to make it. So together, we went in, took him off of the ventilator, and brought him in so that our other kids could meet him and love him. We were beginning the hardest quest of our lives.

We brought our friends and our pastor in to pray with us and to love him. We had him for a couple of hours, and he passed away peacefully right there in our arms. We said goodbye. But at that moment, in the middle of all that, I had never been more overwhelmed.

There will be more than one situation you will walk through where you feel overwhelmed. In those moments, there is usually a crowd of voices in your head (or none at all at the same time), and it feels impossible to make a decision. I felt that way after we left the hospital and we came home. The next day, I got up at 5:00 a.m. It was the day after my son had died, and I didn't know what to do. I was hurting and in shock, and everyone else was asleep. So I went and did the first thing I could think of doing: I mowed the grass. I wanted to get busy, to move, to change my position, and to change my location so that I could start to see it from a different vantage point. And this is exactly what you have to do. In any situation where you feel overwhelmed, you can't stay there because the longer you stay in that overwhelmed space, the more overwhelmed you get. You have to move, you have to get out of that spot, and you need to get to another vantage point so you can start to see things differently.

In the middle of that storm in 2014, we literally just took one day at a time. We would get up on a Monday and handle that day. We would make it to bedtime, and then we would get up on a Tuesday. We'd get through Tuesday, we'd make it to bedtime, and then we'd get up on a Wednesday. Slowly, we made it through each week. And as we made it to the next week, we would get through that, and then we'd make it to the next week. When you're overwhelmed and in the middle of situations that are just so much you can hardly handle them, you take for granted the things that will really push you over the edge. So, go slow and give yourself grace. Give people around you grace when they don't know your full story and all you are going through.

Evans passed away, and we had a burial service on my family's land out in West Texas. After the burial service at the gravesite, we went north on a family trip to Utah. It was beautiful and awful at the same time. We got away with our two older kids to circle the wagons and stay close as a family to process the grief we were going through and to quiet the surrounding noise. We needed less input, and we needed fewer things around us. Often, when you're going through a situation and you feel overwhelmed, you need to turn down the noise. You need to get into a quiet room or just be alone.

You need to intentionally build quiet time into your schedule. (I'm speaking to myself here!) You need to have space for your mind to calm down. You need to have space to get away from the voices for a period and slow down so that you can hear clearly, think about what to do next, take a breath, and actually make a decision.

We returned to town at the end of June and had his funeral at our local church ten days later. Hundreds of our friends, family, and patients came to honor him. It was beautiful and terrible all at the same time, but we just could not have made it without the surrounding community. Right after that, I felt okay and in a good spot, so I went back into the office to start seeing patients again. We ran a busy private practice at the time, and we couldn't afford to have me out for too long. I went back into the office, and I thought I would start seeing some of my routine patients and get back into a rhythm. I'll never forget the day I went back. I remember treating a patient and asking him what was going on. He said something like, "I've just really got this elbow pain in my right arm. This elbow is really bothering me. It's hard for me to get up from a chair and put pressure on it."

And I don't think I have ever felt such rage in my life. I thought, *Really? Your elbow? Like, that's your biggest problem? Your elbow!* I stood behind him and contemplated how hard to hit him to knock him out. It was the closest I'd ever come to punching anyone in my life. I thought, *Well, if I'm about to lose my license for punching a patient, at least it'll free me up from having to be in here. I mean, I wonder if I'll ever be able to get my license again.* All these thoughts went through my mind as he complained about his elbow when I had just buried my son. Luckily, I had enough self-control, and I didn't punch this patient, so it did end on a good note. I just walked right out of the room and closed the door in mid-sentence. I went and got my associate doc and told him what was going on: "I need you to go save this patient's life because if I have to hear about his elbow pain one more time, I think I'm gonna punch him in the face." Dr. Steven and my office manager told me I wasn't ready to be there, so I went home and gave myself another week or two.

Just know that when you're feeling overwhelmed, it takes time to get out of that spot. It takes time to mentally return to where you need to be. Not only do you have to give yourself grace about what you can handle for yourself and where you are to make normal decisions throughout the day, but you have to give other people grace as well. They don't know your story. I mean, a business coach that I used to take classes from always said that at any given time, with anybody that you're around you, you probably only know at most two to five percent of what they're going through in a day.

So if you walk in, others don't know what you're dealing with or what you're feeling. They have no idea what's going on in your marriage unless you've told them. That patient had no idea that I lost a son a week before. And so when he walked in, he walked into the middle of my story. He walked into the middle of my pain. And sometimes we're just so overwhelmed we're on edge.

We have to slow down, back up, and give ourselves space. And again, we have to intentionally put good people in our corner. We have to bring people on the journey with us. We have to have people in our community and on our team who are willing to speak up and hold us accountable. They have to be willing to put up bumpers for us, just like in the bowling alley. That way, we won't run off into the gutter just because we are overwhelmed. You need them to say, "Hey, you need to sit down and breathe into this bag." Or, "Hey, you need to take a mental health day. Or, "Hey, you guys need to talk or journal."

Journaling is what I recommend most when it comes to being overwhelmed. When the mind goes crazy, it's good to get those thoughts out of your head and on the paper to organize them. When we're so overwhelmed after the loss of a loved one or in so much debt, it's hard to know what's true and what's a lie inside your mind. You can convince yourself that the thing that you're going through in your mind is the absolute truth when it's not, and you just need to write things down on paper. You just need to write it down in a journal. Whether you use a bullet journal or a traditional one, write yourself a letter about what's going on in your life.

I've told patients for years that a brain-dump journal methodology is a great way to get all of that out of your mind. So you can write down what you're feeling, what you're thinking, what you're going through in your mind. Then, take a different colored pen and go back through what you wrote and draw a circle around stuff that's really important that you wanna go back to and look at or explore more with your spouse or somebody else that can help. Then, take that same colored pen and draw an X through things that are just complete lies. These are the lies that you're telling yourself or lies that the enemy's trying to get inside your head to discourage you or to get you to quit.

Taking the time to journal like that is really, really important. The best way to get through overwhelming things is to build a margin in your schedule so you can debrief and decompress. Take the time to journal so that you can reset your mind. I've never been great at scheduling and blocking my time out after I got out of private practice because back when I was in private practice and seeing patients all the time, my schedule was pretty much set for me. I saw patients from 7:00 a.m. to noon, then I took a break and made videos and taught online from 12:00 p.m. to 1:00 p.m. After I ate lunch, I saw patients again from 2:00 p.m. to 6:00 p.m. and then did nutritional consultations from 6:00 p.m. to 7:30 p.m. before going home to the kids. It was all set for me. I had to learn a new system in order to make sure that I was scheduling and stewarding my time really well. The one that I love the most that I'm currently using is from a book called *12 Week Year* by Randy Moran. He's got a great system for setting aside and scheduling blocks of time inside your schedule during the week to think, strategize, and rest. That way, you can reset your mind so that you don't become overwhelmed anymore.

What jersey do you need to change in this situation? Are you wearing a jersey of OVERWHELMED? Does your jersey say, "I'm freaking out, I'm overwhelmed, watch out" on the back?

What do you need to switch it to? Maybe you can change it from OVERWHELMED to a jersey that says EXPECTANT on the back. This means being expectant of something good that's going to happen, getting to the end of this, finding a solution, and knowing that good is going to come out of this because you're not going to quit. All you have to do is just keep moving through this valley in order to get to the other side.

Maybe you need to put on a jersey that says EXCITEMENT. Maybe you need to tell yourself, *Hey, I'm not excited about what we went through, but I'm excited about what's coming up.* And it's okay to feel that you're excited about where you are going to be and put that jersey on.

When we're feeling overwhelmed, did you know that there is a hyper innervation (hyper meaning too much) that happens in the nervous system in your brain when your stress hormones get so high? This is due to having such intense stress in the middle of feeling overwhelmed that it puts every single nerve on edge.

Your hormones get out of balance, your blood sugar slows down, all the blood goes from your extremities to your core, and everything starts to get really hyper-focused because your body's one goal in the middle of that stress is just to protect yourself (fight or flight response). And so everything gets on edge, and we need to calm it down. Things that help your nerves really calm down to slow down include:

1. Slow cardio (walking)

2. Breathing exercises are amazing and help to calm the nervous system

3. Infrared sauna

4. Calcium. Make sure you're getting a diet rich in calcium or supplementing with calcium to calm the nerves down.

5. Epsom salt baths are also one of the best ways to give your body the nutrients that you need to calm down.

The key is again to not let it stay that way. The key is to recognize that you're overwhelmed. In order to move out of where you are and get out of being stuck or get out of this position, you have to recognize and realize that you're overwhelmed. Acknowledge that you're overwhelmed. Take the necessary steps, and do the practical things to feed your body so that you can move into another day.

I have a free teaching for you to better understand the fight or flight response and to teach you more about how the Limbic System works,

SCAN THE QR CODE

CHAPTER 4

Shame

During my infidelity in 2011, I hated myself. I hated myself for what I had gotten myself into. I hated myself for what I was doing to my wife and my kids. I hated myself for where I knew that it was probably going to lead, but I also hated myself for the fact that I would have to do so much work to get out of it. I was just buried in shame.

In the middle of that affair, Cindy asked me to move out. We were trying to work through stuff, but I was also a functional alcoholic. Amid the shame I was feeling, I began making worse decisions. Isn't that just like shame? You've lost who you are, and you feel so bad about where you're at or what you've done, and instead of just making better decisions, you make worse ones. Some of it is because you kind of get in the mindset of, *Well, can you really get any worse? What difference does it make now?* In that season, I thought, *I'm going to lose everything. What difference does it make if I'm drinking tonight again?* I know some of you understand that. You've burned everything else down around you, so what's one more thing?

I would leave the office, go to the empty townhouse I was living in, and then I'd stay at the bar and drink at night. After all that, I would get back up and go see patients during the day, and the cycle would repeat. It really only served to numb the feeling that I had of hating everything about where I was and what I was doing. I had to acknowledge how I had actually gotten to that point. It was a slow fade. There's never, in the seasons where you feel ashamed, that it was an instant thing. It's not like you wake up one day and go, *Oh my gosh, I'm ashamed of this!* Shame is something that normally is a series of wrong decisions over the course of years that have gotten you into this situation where you're stuck and don't know how to get out. The shame gets mixed with feeling overwhelmed, and the shame leads us into other things that we know we don't need to be into. Shame pushes you to add insult to injury to try to medicate or soothe that terrible feeling you have. But it only serves to make it all worse.

When you have a failure like that, whether it's personal or a relationship, or it's in your finances, you really have two choices. You can either just get further stuck in the situation you are in and the shame that comes with it, like what we talked about in Chapter 2, or you can get out of it and find another spot.

You can move forward, and you can move through. The pain of getting out of that current spot can be extreme, though. Shame is sticky, and it's painful because it is so personal. I get that when you're in a spot and you feel like you've already made too many bad choices. It feels like you're not gonna be able to get out of this. No one's going to want to stay with me. No one's going to want to do business with me. No one's going to want to stand with me. And I'm here to tell you that's the lie Satan told me during my affair that kept me in it for months longer. I was convinced that I was too far in and too far gone to save my marriage and that if I was honest or tried to fix it, I would lose everything and everyone.

Other people all understand where you're at. Everybody walks through periods of shame. We seclude ourselves because shame takes us away from the community. Shame takes us away from being around people we love who really want to encourage us. And then we have our own little private pity party of one. And that's where shame wants to keep us. To get out of shame, we have to get out of that spot. We have to get into a new spot around people who are encouraging us and helping pull us out of that area.

What cycle are you getting trapped in that's going from shame to bad decision, to shame, to bad decision, and back around? After Cindy and I had gotten back together and made the decision to stay married, we went to counseling and group therapy about the things I had done as we tried to figure out how to piece our marriage back together. When we left the first meeting of this couples counseling group therapy class, Cindy yelled at me in the car about the people that we were there with: "I am in this situation, and I have to be in here with all these perverts because of you!" And it was true.

At first, I was offended. Then I realized, *We are here because of me. We're here because of my choices, but we're gonna get out of here because of me and because of our choices together and we're gonna get to a new spot.* You know, shame also takes on the face of blaming other people and blaming everything around you for where you're at.

One of the best things I ever learned from counseling after our affair came out of working with affairrecovery.com in Austin, Texas. The founder, Rick Reynolds, has an amazing program for people who have gone through infidelity. He has groups for people who committed infidelity and ones who have been cheated on. It's amazing. One of the mantras that they said all the time in our group class was, "My spouse is never my problem. My spouse only reveals the problem within me."

Let me say that again:

***"My spouse is never my problem;
my spouse only reveals the problem within me."***

Meaning, if I came home and Cindy said something and I got mad at her, or I was frustrated with her, or I was disappointed in her, she wasn't actually my problem. She was revealing the problem that was within me. Now you can apply that to everything in your life.

- My kid is never my problem. My kid is only revealing the problem within me. Why am I getting angry? Why am I getting upset? Why am I feeling ashamed of this? It's not them. It's *me*. And that brings all the responsibility back on you in order to feel it.

- My business partner is never my problem. My business partner is only revealing the problem within me.

- My employees are never my problem. My employee is only revealing the problem within me.

- My taxes are not my problem. My taxes only reveal the problem within me.

Do you see how this applies to everything? It takes it from being a blame game and allowing yourself to slip down into this shame cycle and trap that just goes around in a loop and this thing where you hate yourself, and you stay stuck in shame and self-hate. You just keep going right around and around, and it puts the responsibility back on you. What is it in me that is coming out of that, and what do I need to work on, what do I need to fix, what do I need to give up, and what do I need to be open about? What do I need to get help for to move on and be better in this spot?

Another thing that helped me a lot with the shame in different seasons of my life was something a mentor told me. We had been healed for years. Our family had expanded. We were healthy. We were in a very authentic place and had become a strong unit. I was asked to share part of my story at a men's event, and I didn't know what to say. I knew a testimony was so important, but I didn't know what to talk about. I didn't know how to tell people my story. I knew it was important to share because shame can't stay on you if you share it. Shame only stays with you when you hold on to it. When we start to bring people in and tell people what happened and expose it to the light, then shame can't stay there. But the story felt so huge. Even in this book, I've only shared pieces of it. He gave me some advice that stuck with me forever.

So, I asked my mentor what and how I should share with this group. He said, "Just focus on what God did and less on what you did. If you do, they will get it, and you'll be fine." And it was so true, and it focused me back on the testimony of where the Lord had brought us in our marriage, just like it did when he focused me on where he had brought us through the grief of losing our son or the pain that we'd gone through in our finances. When I focused more on what he did and on helping other people where they were and less on what I did and where I was at, it made that shame go away. It gave me purpose again. It gave me something to focus on. It gave me something to come back to. And it gave me something to shoot for and to look ahead at. And that's when it changed for me.

And they overcame him by the blood of the Lamb, and by the word of their testimony; and they loved not their lives unto the death.
– (Revelation 12:11)

It says in Revelation that we will overcome by the blood of the Lamb and the power of our testimony. To get a testimony, you have to go through a test. That's why the test is at the beginning of it. But we overcome with *both*. Some people get stuck in the cycle of begging God to take things away and take things off their plate and then being angry when He doesn't. At the end of it, the Lord's saying, "I'm not taking this away because this is part of your testimony. And on top of just my blood and my salvation, you need your testimony in order to overcome all of this *and* pour into other people coming behind you."

But it doesn't become a testimony until we testify or tell others about it. So part of our calling, part of our responsibility of walking through different seasons in our life, whether it's seasons in our marriage, whether it's seasons in our finances, whether it's seasons in our health or any other season, is to share it with other people. We need to share our successes *and* our failures, our wins *and* our losses.

I'll never forget when one of our favorite midwives, who was a seasoned, experienced, older midwife in the area, came into the office one day to get adjusted after we had lost Evans. I was back in the practice, seeing patients consistently, still grieving and still hurting, but not as overwhelmed and not wanting to punch any patients. So, they were all safe. But back in the office, Betty (not her real name) sat down. I talked to her for just a second, just kind of processing with her. As I was getting ready to adjust to her, she said, "I understand where you're at because I know what you're going through."

I'm sure my shock showed all over my face as I replied, "What do you mean?"

I thought she meant that she just understood from watching people go through it in her profession as a midwife. She stared off into memories and then looked me in the eyes and said, "I lost my first baby. A few hours after delivery, just like yours. There was a genetic issue, and I didn't get to go home with my baby either." It was silent between us as I processed what she was sharing with me because I sensed that she hadn't shared these feelings with many people.

She continued, "There was this hole after that, and it felt like I was missing a leg. I didn't think that I was ever going to get out of it. You never really get over it, but you will get through it." It felt like a seasoned warrior pouring out her wisdom to a rookie. She knew it wouldn't be the only war I would face.

She said, "The pain will always stay there at some point, but you'll get through it, and it won't hurt the same. You'll be able to help other people as you get through this." She nodded and smiled as tears ran down my face. I hugged her, adjusted her, and we parted ways.

Who comforteth us in all our tribulation, that we may be able to comfort them which are in any trouble, by the comfort wherewith we ourselves are comforted of God.
– (2 Corinthians 1:4)

I never forgot her words. I've repeated them to hundreds of people face to face as they've sat in front of me and cried. I've taught them to thousands of people from the stage. You'll never get over some of the things you have experienced. And why would you want to?

Why would I want to get over my son's life?! I don't want to get over him. But I did want to get through the sharp pain and the fresh wound his loss left in me. You will get through the feelings that you're feeling right now, and you will get through this shame.

You can and will get through this feeling and the pain of feeling like you're a failure in this fight and the shame of what you've done or the shame of where you're at or the shame of what happened. You will get through it, even if you don't ever get over it, because you need to learn from it. And that is the key.

And you never know if a comment or a statement you make to somebody is exactly what they need to hear to change their life forever. That's why it's so important for us to push through and work on healing from our own struggles. If we never heal, if we never get out of the shame, we never get out of the overwhelm, and we just sit down where we're at, then we're never able to turn around and tell people what we've done from a place of authority and experience. At this point, we're just telling them what we're walking through, but we're in the same thing they're at and can't help them. And it's really hard to pull somebody out of the mud pit that you're lying in, too. It's almost impossible.

If you're sitting in the middle of this bucket of shame with someone else, you're not going to be able to pull that person out. You gotta get out first. You gotta get out of that mud, pit, or quicksand and pull yourself to help the other person out. It's important to be able to think about those things and speak to people from experience. But even though you need to be out of the mud pit to pull someone else out, you don't have to have all the mud washed off of you to do it. Don't be paralyzed into not helping people because you feel like you have to be perfectly clean to speak into anyone else's experience. That's not true.

Jersey Exchange

So what jersey are you wearing?

Are you wearing a jersey that says ASHAMED on the back?

Is your jersey part of your scarlet letter? Do you have your sin or failure on the back? Does it proclaim ADULTERER, SINNER, LIAR, or CHEATER because you're just ashamed of the thing that you've done?

Well, you get to exchange it.

How about you exchange that jersey from SHAME to one that says FORGIVEN? You can put on a jersey that says REDEEMED or RESTORED. That's a jersey that actually truly defines where you're at and your potential. That's a jersey that really makes a difference. That's a jersey that points to the future and doesn't dwell on the past because we can't focus on the past if we're going to get into the future; you can't focus on what happened then to get to where you are now.

Nerd Depot: The Science

Let's look at the way the brain is wired and how it functions when we experience shame. With shame, you fire an exorbitant amount of stress hormone cortisol, and once this hormone is fired for so long, it will start to create a pathway that makes it to where your body starts to feel shame quicker and believes it is a part of you. Shame isn't a normal emotion, so why do we battle it so much?

Did you know you can create a stress response inside the brain with just a thought? Because of how impactful the emotions really are, we don't even have to go through the experience to create the hormone and the stress and subsequent damage. The main area of the brain that stores negative emotions and negative situations is called the amygdala, also called "The Seat of Emotions." The amygdala stores an experience as a file and sends information to your limbic system that tries to keep you from falling into that same trap again. It tries to keep you from allowing people to hurt you or keep you from wherever you were that felt that pain. As a result, you can stay in this reactive, protective loop for years if you don't recognize it. It can turn you into the person who tries to avoid experiences instead of embracing them to learn from them or enjoy them.

What can you do?

Some of the best things you can do is just talk about the experience or situation to reset your brain. Other things like movement, walking, and exercise create enough change in your neurology to help reset that broken record and get you out of that pathway or rut. Journaling is really important, too, because you're able to get those feelings of shame or guilt down on paper and then write the truth off to the side. Physically verbalizing through a pen, *I feel ashamed about this over here, but the truth is, that was a mistake. It's not who I am. The choices I make aren't who I am. I am now this person on the right. I'm making new decisions, and I'm doing new things. Those decisions aren't gonna define me.*

Another therapy that we recommend is called "Brain Tap." It is an app on your phone that actually has a visual system (think virtual reality like Oculus Quest) that you wear that utilizes light frequency to help calm the brain down. When you're dealing with major emotions like shame, using something that is really neurologically based, like Brain Tap, can help to unlock those pathways that the brain is stuck in and get your body into a place of relaxation and peace to be able to reset, let it go, and move on. And that's the key, making the choice to let it go and move on, or you're gonna stay there. Let's make the choice to change and move forward. I know it's scary, but I'll jump with you.

I have a free gift for you with this QR code.
I want to connect you to an amazing community and resources to help you remember WHO you are!

SCAN THE QR CODE:

CHAPTER 5

Anxiety

I grew up being more arrogant and proud than anxious. I never really understood anxiety. To be completely honest, until I was an adult, I thought anxiety was a weakness. I just always thought, *Just stop being anxious!* I've had to repent for that as an adult. I never really fully got it. I never fully understood because I was so proud. I looked at that group of people that dealt with anxiety as either lazy and didn't wanna work on it, or they were just weak and they couldn't. And so I never connected with it until 2017, when I shattered my femur.

In the spring of 2017, I was in full-time chiropractic practice and also traveling and speaking at events and conferences around the country every week. We were in Florida when I started experiencing swelling in my left leg. It bothered me, but I chalked it up to just traveling and being on airplanes, eating airport food, and sleeping in weird beds and didn't think anything about it. I even sent myself in for an MRI of my ankle, which is where the swelling and discomfort mainly were, but I never looked anywhere else. I went against everything I told patients in my office for years.

We ended up in Orlando at a big conference there with people from all over the world. Before it started, since I had Cindy and our four kids with me, I wanted to be a super fun dad. (Can't you see me in my superhero outfit? No, just me? Hmmm.) Harper, my oldest, was nine at the time and wanted to go on the FlowRider, which is a surfing simulator at the Orlando Gaylord Hotel. So being a fun dad, I was like, "Yes, let's do this!" We went down there, signed up, and signed the liability waivers, which were rather long and lengthy (which should have been my first clue, my first warning).

After we signed the liability waivers and got into this thing, Harper—being a little athletic 10-year-old—hopped in, did a surfing move, rolled around, and looked amazing, like he was on *Hawaii Five-0*. Then it was my turn. I got up there, and the 18-year-old surf pro running the ride said, "Start here on this side, and you're going to walk your way into the current from right to left, as the current comes right at you. (Said in my best surfer accent... "It was tubular.")

As I walked into the current, I just remember taking three steps in holding this little boogie board, and all of a sudden, everything in me just screamed, *NOOOO!* and that I shouldn't do this. I decided to bail and just flop on my rear like a fat kid and roll out and not do this, but at that, the current washed my left foot out from under me, and as my leg twisted and it started to sprain my ankle, I over corrected and it bent my leg out to the side. Well, what I didn't know at that time was I had a benign tumor that had grown inside that femur, and that leg was hollow, so when it bent the leg out, it shattered my femur, ripped off half my knee, and washed me over to the side of the surfing simulator, like a rag doll.

My entire world shattered, just like my femur. I ended up in massive allograft surgery, years of rehab, testing to make sure that the tumor was benign and not malignant, and a direction that ended up taking me out of private chiropractic practice altogether.

While I was in the emergency room in Florida, the hospital gladly put me in a leg brace to keep it completely immobilized and asked me to leave. They wanted nothing to do with that leg. So a buddy of mine flew in from Kansas City, rented a car, and—along with three of my other friends—loaded me into the back seat of that Suburban and drove me the 16-plus hours home. After we got home, reality set in quickly. My leg was shattered, and we had four *little* kids. We set up appointments with specialists in Fort Worth and had a transport take me there while Cindy gathered herself and figured out help with the kids. It took a month after all the testing and diagnosis for the orthopedic oncologist here in Fort Worth to decide how to fix it because it was such a massive injury.

For a month, when I got home, I had a shattered leg and a leg immobilizer. I was on pain meds and laid up in bed or on the couch with four little kids. It was terrifying. That was the first time that I understood what anxiety truly felt like and what anxiety truly was because anytime they touched my foot, that shattered leg would contract and spasm the muscles around my femur. It was the most excruciating thing I'd ever experienced in my life, to the point of wanting to pass out. Over the course of that month, that anxiety started building up from the pain and unknown, but also, it was as if when I shattered my femur, my arrogant naivety about everything always being fine shattered along with it.

Before I had surgery and I was in a wheelchair, we took the kids to the park by our house, where a huge playground was. I had a full-on panic attack watching my kids on the playground because I no longer believed that it was going to be fine if my then two-year-old was at the very top of this playground. I immediately saw them falling off in my mind and breaking an arm, a leg, or their neck, or having a closed head injury. I saw all the scenarios in my mind of what could happen and how far it was before I could get there, how long it would take us to get back in the car, how many miles it was to the hospital, how long it would take to get there, knowing how fast they would bleed out (doctor brain) and how much brain damage they would have, how many deficits they were probably going to live with and knowing that we would have a quadriplegic son for the rest of our life, all from sitting in front of that playground. (Phew, my heart rate goes up just thinking about it.)

That was when I first finally understood what anxiety feels like. Then, I had to apologize to all the people that I had previously judged. Because in different modes in your life, when you hit that spot, and you have actual anxiety coming on, your brain has gotten into a rut, and your neurology is out of balance. You've done things that have gotten you out of the path you're supposed to go for long enough that your brain and your body and your neurology freak out, and now these extra stimuli become anxiety. It's hard, it feels overwhelming, and it feels like it's an insurmountable mountain that you really can't get over because your body wants to shut down and stop.

Well, the thing that you need to hear is sometimes anxiety comes on because of things that you've done and made choices about, but that overwhelming feeling isn't your fault. It's just your body reacting to the situation you're in. It is your brain doing what it's supposed to do to keep you safe. Sometimes, you build up anxiety from things that happened to you that you had no control over, like my leg or my business deals. That initial feeling or emotion is a normal response from the body to protect you and slow you down. It's designed to give you caution. But if left, it can control your entire life.

Another thing I do—that is a passion of mine—is business coaching. I work with small to medium businesses and business owners to build and launch their businesses and navigate the world as an entrepreneur. There's one business owner that I worked with who was a brand-new entrepreneur. Less than a year into starting his business, his partner quit on him, and he started having massive anxiety. Fear came up because his stability—this person, who was supposed to walk this out *with* him—had walked *out* on him. That hurt a lot. And if you have been in business for yourself and had that happen (I have!), it can be super scary. That happened *to* him. It wasn't something that he tried to do. It wasn't something that he had planned for. People getting sick or things happening around you that come into your sphere and into your environment are not your fault.

It's not your fault. It's not something that you wanted or created. The first thing that I would do is step back, take a breath, and say to myself, *It's okay that I'm feeling this way. It's not my fault that it's happening, and there is hope. This is my body protecting itself, and there is hope that I will get out of this.* The biggest thing that happens when you start with anxiety is this imbalance in the brain, but when the anxiety gets worse, it can lead to other neurological and psychological issues that we'll get into in the following chapters that are harder to dig out of. But no matter how far along in this journey of life you're going, no matter how far in your marriage, no matter how far in your finances, no matter how far in all of these different things you are, as dark as it seems, there is hope.

And that's what you need to hear. There's hope for you to be able to make a new path. There's hope for you to calm down the anxiety and get a plan. There's hope for you to stop that sense of overwhelm when your brain sees everything and doesn't know how to focus on one thing. When you see your two-year-old at the top of that playground, and you're terrified that they're going to fall down, when before you were always the fun dad taking them to the top of the playground, there is always hope for you to be able to course correct.

Max Lucado wrote the book *You'll Get Through This*, and it was really helpful in helping me understand this part about being okay. I picked it up and read it in the wake of losing our son. And in his book, he talks about the concept of just understanding that no matter what you are going through, you will get through it. It's the nature of the human experience, and it's the nature of what we go through. He says that throughout the course of his career as a pastor and as a traveling speaker and author, he's had countless people come up to him and tell him things that they went through in their lives, from the loss of family members to anxiety to whatever it was. And he said he's told all of them the exact same thing: "I don't know how, I don't know when, and I don't know how long it'll take, but I do know that you'll get through this."

And this is the premise of the entire book. You have to hear this and own it. You *will* get to the other side of this. And taking this part of anxiety and realizing that anxiety is a response in the body, and it is a neurological protective mechanism that your body is going through just to protect you. You can't own that, though. You can't own that neurological symptom as your identity. You can't wear that as a jersey. You can't wear anxiety as, *Hey, I have anxiety, I am anxiety, I am anxious.* That's the jersey that people will put on. And so if that's a jersey that you're wearing, and it's something that you're putting on, then you will start to see the rest of the world in every single situation and every single event, through that lens.

Understanding what's true and not true when you're dealing with anxiety around business decisions or in your marriage is one of the most powerful steps you can take and one of the hardest at the beginning because when you're in the middle of that anxiety, everything feels like the truth. Everything you see feels like truth, and to you, to the person who is dealing with the anxiety, dealing with seeing these things in it that are overwhelming your entire system, is truth to you. That whole perception is your reality and you're perceiving these events as being catastrophic, whether it's with your finances, your family, or your business. And you're seeing this business move as catastrophic, or this loss of a client as catastrophic because you know how much that they bring into the company. But instead of focusing on the growth, the positive, or what can go right, your brain will quickly and immediately go to what is wrong and what will go wrong. Your body is literally trying to pre-protect you. It's trying to prepare you for all of these things because one of the things that your body realizes and one of the things that your brain knows is that if it can prepare for it, at least on that end, you're not surprised. Right? At least it's not this big shocker, which is more stressful and scary, right?

My brain thinks that if it can prepare me for somebody to jump out behind a door and scare me, I'll be less scared because I'm prepared. And it will be far better than if I'm walking along and all of a sudden they just jump out, and they ambush me.

Jersey Exchange

Does the jersey you are currently wearing have ANXIOUS or ANXIETY on the back?

Have you allowed your body to be overtaken by the fear and the "what ifs"? Can you see a hundred different options or possibilities and can't make a decision? Do you feel trapped? Are you dealing with paralysis by analysis and finding it difficult to move forward? If this is you and you're wearing the ANXIOUS jersey, it's time to exchange it for COURAGE or DECISIVENESS. One of the things that helps the most in moving forward is being able to discern between what is true and what is not. Then, just take a step forward to do the next best thing. Even if it's a small step, forward progress is progress forward.

Each jersey comes with glasses that you see the world through because they create a certain reality for you based on that jersey. You become what you *see*. And so every single thing becomes an anxious perspective. Here are some:

- Oh my gosh, it's probably going to happen like [X] (always bad).
- I wish I could be positive, but I'm sure that it's gonna fail.
- I'm sure they're gonna leave me.
- I'm sure this isn't gonna work out.
- I'm sure this diagnosis isn't gonna heal.
- I'm sure this is going to go on forever.

If anxiety builds up and you consistently practice the wrong steps, it can lead to more serious psychological and mental issues.

Nerd Depot: The Science

When I was dealing with anxiety, I worked with a practitioner who did EFT (Emotional Freedom Technique). It's a more natural way to use tapping, pressure points, and essential oils to reset a broken record of stress in your brain and allow your brain and nervous system to breathe so that you can differentiate the anxiety and the lies in your mind from the truth. I did a couple of treatments with her and talked through what it meant and what I was feeling. We did some affirmations, worked on some pressure points, and went through the process in my brain of what was going on. I was able to objectively look at what I was feeling to see if it was true. I asked myself, *What's actually going on? And is this really gonna happen? Is this really something that I need to be concerned about? Or is this my brain running wild and creating a false sense of reality, this false thing that can't really happen?* It gave me something to hold on to. I started using affirmations and some words. I was journaling to be able to make sure that I could differentiate the truth from the lie inside my mind.

At the end of this chapter, there's a QR code that you can use to access a mini course I created around brain balancing and anxiety, so you can see how an imbalance in the way that the brain communicates can create anxiety or make your brain see things a certain way. Neurology looks at the two halves of your brain or parietal lobes, which give you different mental programming around any scenario that you're walking into, so they see the world differently.

Everyone has a different brain balance and a way they normally operate. These usually map up pretty closely. I wanna go into this briefly so you can understand the way that the brain works and give you some practical tools to feed the brain correctly and help it bounce back if you get too far out of balance.

The right side of the brain is your more creative side. It's your more colorful, artistic, and musical side. It's the side of the brain that is more loving, doting, and empathetic, kind of like your caring side (think momma bear brain). Extreme right brain activity that's out of balance leads to anxiety. You see everything, but you can't really make a decision. You see everything, all the color, but you can't see the steps to the solution.

The left side of the brain is your mathematical side, the more engineering, black and white, top to bottom, left to right side. It's the part of the brain that contains more testosterone receptors. It's the side of the brain you use to make and store memories. You make decisions on more of the left side of the brain. And it is the side of the brain that, if it is overactive, leads to action without consequence. You'll lose emotion, and you do more things to people or around people with no regard for their feelings. You become a jerk, in a sense, from overactivity on the left side of the brain.

The perfection of the creation of our neurology is that you get to operate in both. You make decisions on the left with emotion on the right. You get to paint and create music on the right while doing math on the left. You get to have fun and be creative and all these things while having order and organization. You have access to both sides of the brain, so why not use it?

Now, with the Enneagram or the disc assessment, you can map personality, but a lot of people are just naturally more on one side or the other. I am mostly balanced left to right, maybe slightly more right-brain dominant at times, but I am equal enough on both sides that I can enjoy order and lists and journaling and lined paper for my left side of the brain, and love music, being crazy, and the blank paper for the right side of my brain. If you love to highlight everything and draw all over your notes and use colored pens—I have a stack of colored pens right here as I'm writing this book—you're more right-brain dominant. (Shout out to all my creatives!) If you love whiteboards, blank things, creating stuff, being vision-driven, and seeing all the things, you're probably more right-brain dominant.

Now, if you have a hard time with that and you wanna see one step at a time, you're mathematically or results-driven, you don't like a lot of colors, you wear mainly black and white or grays, everything has to be very organized, and you get anxious when things are out of order, you're probably more left-brained. Both are beautiful and perfect.

We are meant to have a blend of both sides. The key is to stay in your normal balance and function the way you're supposed to. If you understand this concept (or the basics), then you can automatically remember that if/when you feel anxiety coming on, you know it is the right side of your brain over-firing. That gives us the option to do something to help our brain balance no matter whether you're a typically left-brain dominant person or more creative. If there's too much right brain activity, then you will create more anxiety, and your body will start to feel and focus on that. It'll increase stress hormones and estrogen release in the body. It'll increase blood sugar dysregulation. It'll increase inflammation inside your body while slowing down digestion.

All these things will happen at the exact same time. So if there's an anxious situation at work and your stomach is bothering you, it's not because you've got a virus. It's because you are just dealing with so much neurological stress it will affect your digestive system. If you have too much right brain activity, you can get what is known as Irritable Bowel Syndrome (IBS).

Irritable Bowel Syndrome is very commonly caused by an overactive right brain and sympathetic nervous system, which is your stress response in the brain and leads to diarrhea and constipation. (Side note: In medical talk, if they call something a syndrome, it's usually code for a pile of symptoms they don't know the origin of, so they put them in a big basket. End rant.) A woman came up to me at an event where I was talking about how brain balance and anxiety will stop you in your tracks and not allow you to move forward in life.

I was speaking at an event about this very topic when this woman came up to me. She was dressed in a professional suit like an executive and carried herself really well, but she was crying. She said to me, "I need your help with this." She told me she worked about an hour and a half away from home in a downtown area as vice president of this big corporation. Her anxiety was so high it was affecting her gut so much that on the way to work, she couldn't control it anymore. She would have to stop two times in traffic on her way to work to go to the bathroom on the side of the road in her expensive suit.

Once I gave her practical tools, her body healed itself. She stopped having to stop on the side of the road, her digestive system calmed down, and her body was able to handle it better. It completely changed her life. The key is to look at your diet and make sure you're eating the things that you're supposed to and getting plenty of protein, water, and healthy fats. The main thing you want to avoid is too much sugar and artificial sweeteners. They directly attack and damage your neurological tissue.

The QR code below will give you lots of practical tips, from easy exercises to essential oils, that will help calm your system down, give you clarity so that you can then decide what is true, and make a better decision based on things so that you're not stuck in anxiety but moving forward in confidence.

I have two free gifts for you with this code.
I want to give you a course on Brain Balancing AND my course on Anxiety. You're not alone, friend.

SCAN THE QR CODE:

CHAPTER 6

Depression

In the last chapter, we talked about anxiety and how an overactive right brain can stop you from making decisions. If you don't get it under control, the next step can be a feeling of depression. This is why I'm encouraging you to take steps to realize where you are, recognize the jersey you're wearing, and identify anything that's currently holding you back from moving forward.

If we don't make a change in Chapter 5, depression is the next step in the neurological progression. In life, when things begin to feel hopeless, it can seem like there's no way out. There are neurological and psychological reasons why a lot of people tend toward depression, and the statistics of depression in the United States are unbelievable, particularly among teenagers. But the main reason the slippery slope towards depression starts has nothing to do with a massive imbalance in neurotransmitters in their brain at the beginning. It has to do with an imbalance in diet, purpose, and anxiety they either never acknowledged or left alone for a long enough period that it turned into depression. Depression feels like you are in a dark room where someone has shut off all the lights or blacked them out, and there's no way out.

People can react very differently in this situation. Some people, when they feel hopeless, just quit doing everything and freeze. They want to give up and the fear and despair of not wanting to do the wrong thing or make things worse keeps them where they are.

The second group of people in this situation start banging into every wall, and they overreact and overcompensate for feeling hopeless. In the middle of that overcompensation, they make a bigger problem than what was already there before. Both of these choices, when you're in the middle of this dark room, are incorrect. Both choices can land you in a lot of trouble. If you're in a spot in your marriage, and you know that there's no way out, doing nothing is not the answer. At the same time, over-responding, doing too much, and becoming desperate can create more problems than it fixes. The best thing you can do is to start slowly and begin feeling your way around that room. (When you read "room," think *marriage,* or *finances,* or *job,* or wherever you are, that feels dark.)

In life, there's always a window somewhere in that room. There's always a doorway somewhere in that room. Have you ever done an Escape Room challenge? In this, they lock you and your friends in a room and then give you clues to get yourself out. You have to work together to solve it. Depression can be a very similar feeling. The only difference is in the escape room, the lights are on, and you have to decipher clues. When you are feeling hopeless, it *feels* like a completely dark room, but there are no riddles. All we have to do is move around to figure out where the door or window is. And we've got to take our time and figure out where it is so that we can get to that room or window and open the blinds to shine a little light in there. If we can get to the door and figure out how to make another decision, we can get out of that room. Otherwise, you get stuck in a loop. If you stay in the middle of that dark room and you never do anything else, you get stuck.

Where you are right now is just where you are right now, but you don't have to stay there. There are so many seasons in life where you're going to feel stuck, but this is just where you currently are.

Always remind yourself:

This is just where I am right now, and the things that I'm experiencing are where I am, but that's not where I have to stay, and that's not where I'm going to always be.

There are a couple of different analogies, but one I've taught for a long time is about the valley and the mountains. When you're on a mountaintop, everything feels like it's going great. Everything's amazing; you have the Midas touch, and everything you touch turns to gold; every business deal is successful; everything that you and your wife do just feels like a honeymoon; your kids always listen to you, and everything works well for you. Life is easy and you're just rolling, but it's hard to focus on growing in those seasons. It's really hard to get better in those seasons because it feels like there is less need.

When you get off that mountain and into the valley, it feels really lonely. It's really daunting, and it feels like you're never going to get out of it. This is the area where you grow. But people tend to panic and think, *Oh man, this is it. I'm just going to stay here.* And they start to get discouraged. (All of us do it; it's human nature.) A valley is only a valley if there's a mountain on either side. If you come off into a low spot, it's not a valley but a plain. The plains of life can seem to go on forever, and that's not the way that life is made. Life has ups and downs. There are valleys and mountains and valleys and mountains. This is the way God has designed the journey of our lives. Highs and lows. Mountains and valleys. So, the only way that you don't get to the next mountain, the only way that you don't go up to a higher level, the only way that you don't improve in your marriage, in your parenting, or in your life, is if you stay in the valley and you sit down and you stop walking. The only way that you don't improve and get out of it is if you don't move ahead. Sitting there can't be an option because if we sit down in the middle of the valley, we're never going to get to the other side.

One of my favorite authors is Charlotte Gambill. Her book *Miracle in the Middle: Finding God's Voice in the Void* speaks about this exact concept. Maybe she got the concept from me! LOL. In her book, she talks about hallways and doorways. She talks about the only way that you don't get to the next doorway in life is if you sit down in the hallway, and you don't get up and you don't keep moving. She talks about a concept exactly like what I've talked about in the valley of moving through the hallways and getting through the hallways quickly so that you can get to the next doorway.

When we lost Evans in June 2014, it felt like the longest valley in creation. If I'm being honest, some days we are still in that valley. There's not a day that goes by that we don't think about him, and there's not a time where it still doesn't hurt knowing that he's not here. In order to help someone else, you need to move through the emotions and walk through that whole valley. Cindy and I have talked a lot about how people deal with hard things differently. Cindy and I are drastically different in this area.

Some of you guys reading this are more like me. You want to jump into it; you want to roll around in the pain or grief or change, and you want to figure it out and understand it all. You want to hear about the valley, research the valley, get mad, have emotions, and then take off running through the valley (sometimes rushing, but that's okay) and just move. Your entire personality has been built around figuring it all out. And that's how I respond to things that are difficult or to tragedy. That doesn't mean I always made the right decisions, but I'm always wanting to move.

Cindy responds totally differently. She processes things slower because every step in that valley makes her mad. Every step into that valley, grief, or frustration in parenting, makes her mad. It's frustrating for her, and she has to really wrap her mind around it and has to finally give in to it to accept it and move forward. She also wants to understand it, but in a deeper way, and won't move forward until she knows everything about all of her options. She wants to have a good, better, best scenario and look at every possibility before she decides.

Both perspectives are perfectly healthy and normal because they actually involve you moving forward. There are downsides to both types of personalities in this as well, and that's where your community and the people around you help you so much. She helps me slow down, and I help her speed up. It's a balance. It doesn't matter how fast you get through the valley. It just matters that you get through the valley. It doesn't matter how great you look on the other side of the valley and how good your makeup and your hair look. It just matters that you get through the valley.

In our experience, the number one thing that has gotten us through our valley, especially in losing our son, is walking together and having other people walking with us. Now, they may be in a jeep. Let's say you're going through your valley and it's your valley to go through, but now and then there are people who come through that have been through this valley before. Now they're kind of tour guides in this valley, and they roll up and say, "Hey, we've been in this valley, and we know there's a bunch of quicksand up ahead, so why don't you hop in the jeep and we'll take you around it?" It's still your choice, my choice, or Cindy's choice to move ahead and accept help in different areas when you feel like there's nothing else you can do to keep moving forward.

The valley isn't easy, and it isn't fun most of the time. The DEPRESSED or HOPELESS jersey is hard to take off. When that jersey goes on, the number one thing that it takes for you to move ahead and change is humility. Humility is realizing, *Hey, you know what, I'm not as cool as I thought I was, and this is harder than I thought it was going to be.* Or, *Wow, this is gonna take longer than I thought it would, and this is a lot more work, and I'm not as equipped as I thought I was.* Maybe you are not as smart as you thought you were, and not as ready as you had hoped you were, and that is okay. Acknowledging where you are and having the humility to call it out and ask for help is an enormous step toward victory and progress. That means being able to look up at your friend in the tour jeep and admit, "I'm actually not doing as well as I thought I was, and I need some help, so can I hop in the jeep with you?" Allowing them to take you the distance to the next step takes a lot of humility.

Your friends won't be able to take you all the way out of your valley (even though that would be magical), but they can take you to the next checkpoint. And then you get to do more work and more digging and exploration into where you are and where you need to be. You need to ask the Lord to go deeper in that area, helping you to dig up more wounds and allowing them to heal slowly. Again, remember, if you come off of a mountain and you find yourself in a valley, you gotta just keep walking. And as you're in that valley, who are you reaching out to? Who is in your support center? Who is in the circle that you would like to reach out to who knows you directly or doesn't? Who are your mentors in this season?

I have been mentored by people who have never known my name, from John Maxwell to Jon Gordon to Jon Acuff. (Obviously, I like guys named John.) I have learned from the books of Craig Groeschel, Steven Furtick, and other authors who have helped me walk through valleys.

They have helped me to grow and figure out why I was in the valley, what got me into the valley, and to become someone new to get out.

Once you own the fact that you're there to learn and understand, ask yourself, *How did I get here?* Sometimes, someone drops you in the valley: Maybe your business partner pulls out and tanks your entire business, and you go from the mountaintop to the valley, but you didn't choose to be there. You got dropped out of a helicopter into that valley. But sometimes, it's your decisions that got you into the valley: You took a wrong turn, and instead of your jeep going up the side of this mountain, you nosedived into the valley. But work out how you got there and what you have to do to get out because you don't want to be the same person on the other side of the valley that you were when you got in. I don't want to get to the other side of the valley and go up that second mountain and be the exact same person who will have to pull myself out of another valley. I want to go up another mountain. I want that next mountain to be more amazing. And the valley that I'm most likely going to get into next will be shorter and not as low. I want to improve.

In the middle of the valley, you have a chance to reflect, look deep, and ask yourself, *How did I get here? How did we get here as a family? How did we get here as a business? And what is it going to take to get to the other side? Who do I need to be to lead my people through this to the other side to get to that other thing?* Moses had to go through a valley and a desert for 40 years before he was ready to take the Israelites to the promised land. Once he heard the Lord's voice in the burning bush, the Lord told him to go to Egypt and tell Pharaoh to let His people go.

Right after that, he walked away and spent forty years in the desert, his valley, not because the Israelites weren't ready to get out but because Moses wasn't equipped to get there yet. Part of the journey of the valley is understanding where you are and understanding who you need to become, through knowledge and growth, to be the person who can take your group to the next level. Take a look at your inner circle. Are the people around you leading you through your valley, or are the people around you keeping you in your valley? Are the people around you pointing you toward the next mountain or dragging you back to the mountain you just came from? Are the people pushing you forward, or are the people pushing you back?

One of my favorite kids' movies is *The Croods*. I love kids' movies. I think there's inspiration in most of them. I'm the annoying dad at every movie theater, clapping loudly, and going, "Yes! YES! That's it! That's amazing! Come on!" LOL. I write notes down in these kids' movies because of their revelations. In *The Croods*, they're following a guy named Guy (genius, I know, and the sister is called Eep). And they are running away from the end of the world, and they're "following the sun to tomorrow." It's totally prophetic. I love this movie. At one point, they're on one side of what's effectively the Grand Canyon. They're getting ready to go over to the other side, and the mom gets scared.

People can try to keep you in your valley because they get scared. Maybe they're scared of progress or of what could happen on the other side because while it hurts in the valley and it's hard, it's also familiar. Sometimes familiarity is more comfortable, even when it isn't good. And so, moving out of the valley, you can feel afraid of what could be on the other side. What if it's worse? What if there's not a mountain? What if it's a ravine? And so they try to hold you back, or your own fears hold you back.

In the movie, they get to the edge of this ravine, and they need to get over to the other side, but there are volcanoes, and everything's happening—the world's ending, and all this stuff is crashing around them. And the mom says, "We can't do this, we can't go across. We need to go back to our cave!" They had been raised in a cave, and they were taught that anything outside of the cave was bad and that they would die if they went outside. And so the movie was about them not dying and fighting fear. It was about them not pressing into who they were supposed to be because of fear.

While the mom is pulling on the dad and the brother, the daughter pulls away and says, "No, no. We need to go this way."

The mom says, "No, we could die!" (Are you feeling the tension yet?)

The daughter stops and says quite forcefully, "NO! Not dying is NOT living!"

It gets me every time. It's a thing that I've taught at events over and over and over again. So many people are afraid to get to that next mountain and walk through their valley because they're afraid of dying instead of focusing on living. The daughter doesn't want to go back to the cave. They figure out how to get across the ravine, and they all live. The other side of the ravine is an amazing oasis of beauty; it's basically the Garden of Eden. They all live and change their legacy to focus on living because they decided to get to the other side instead of being afraid of what could come up. It's an amazing movie. You gotta see it, even though I already told you the ending. (Sorry, not sorry.) If you have seen it, you need to go see it again. Maybe I'll do a course on *The Croods*.

Who is in your circle? Who's pulling you back? Who's moving you forward? You may have to walk away from some relationships that aren't feeding you and pushing you in the direction you need to go. You may have to make some hard decisions and put up some boundaries with people who aren't helping you walk through your valley. Some people get so distraught and stressed out in the middle of the valley and the middle of dealing with this type of jersey of depression or hopelessness that they start meandering or going in circles trying new things and get-rich-quick schemes, instead of just doing what they should in order to budget, go straight, keep moving forward and holding fast to the values and habits that are right. They want to try every quick-help thing for their marriage. They want to try every fad diet for their health. They want to try every lotion and potion for their health instead of just doing the next thing that they were created to do, being consistent, and moving ahead. And just like someone pulling you backward, someone who is dealing with that amount of hopelessness and fear is never gonna get out of the valley by running around in circles. And so you may have to set up boundaries and back away from certain people and put people in place in your life in order to move ahead, right?

Jersey Exchange

What jersey are you wearing? Does your jersey say DEPRESSED or HOPELESS on it? If it does, then it's stealing all the joy from your life. If you're going to change that jersey, let's take off that DEPRESSED jersey and put on the one that says HOPE or HOPEFUL.

Nerd Depot: The Science

Looking at the science of this and focusing on the way that your body is made, understand that the hopelessness and overwhelming feelings you have are the end result of the fight or flight response of your brain. The hormones have been pumping for so long that your body gets overwhelmed and exhausted. It will no longer fire the same, and you don't have the same blood sugar regulation. You could have some long-term exhaustion settling in, adrenal fatigue, and endocrine disruption.

In this situation, the best thing you can do is focus on what you can control. The two easiest things to control in this scenario are your diet and movement. Put things into your diet to help balance blood sugar and help move you forward, like really good protein and fats. At the same time, take out the things that are going to cause more blood sugar issues and anxiety, like artificial sugars, excess sugar, and excess carbs.

You also need to be intentional about getting consistent movement by doing basic activities such as marching in place, cross-crawl exercises, sitting on an exercise ball, bouncing on a rebounder trampoline, walking, rucking, cycling, or rowing. These are things that provide consistent movement to help balance your brain, emotions, and hormones to help move you in the right direction. Remember, these emotions aren't wrong; it's what we do with them and what we allow them to do to us that ends up creating long-term issues and long-term symptoms. So change your jersey, focus on the next best thing, and get through that valley to the other mountain.

I have some amazing tips and resources to help you with your fitness.

We also have a 6-week fitness challenge for you!

SCAN THE QR CODE:

CHAPTER 7

Wanting to quit

"To quit or not to quit?" This *can't* be the question…

I hope one of the things you've picked up throughout this book is that it is okay to feel what you're feeling. The emotions you're feeling, the anxiety you might feel, the depression you might have gotten into, the shame of where you're at, all of these things are okay to feel. It's just not okay to let it keep you where you are. It's not okay to stay that way. You have to be okay with what they are, acknowledge the emotion for what it is, and then work out a plan to get to the next phase. Otherwise, you will want to quit.

In the fall of 2023, my mom rang as we were coming back from vacation in early November to say my dad was talking funny. Some weird speech issues had come up. He wasn't making sense, he was writing weird words, and my initial fear was that he was having a stroke. Cindy and I were headed back from a trip in Oklahoma (which had been a mess with Cindy passing kidney stones while pregnant—not fun), so it was going to be a few hours before we made it back home. I told my mom to head to the emergency room at the hospital in Fort

Worth. I would get everybody home and unpacked and would meet her there. I told her to tell them when she arrived that she was afraid that he was having a stroke.

She was scared but agreed, so I hung up. I prayed with Cindy in the car about it, and then we headed home and got settled. After this, I went to meet them at the ER. The staff had done a CT scan on my dad's head, and the doctor returned with two or three interns and nurses, none of whom looked happy, which is never a good sign. (Pro tip: if you are ever in the hospital and a whole group comes in to give you the results of your test or scans, brace yourself.) The doctor said, "Mr. Haggerton, we got the scans back, and the good news is your dad's not having a stroke, and there are no cardiovascular issues." I was relieved but knew there had to be more to the story, so I waited before I responded. Then he said, "But he does have a very large tumor on the left side of his brain, and I don't think it's the primary tumor."

I knew what he was trying to tell me, so I asked him, "So you think this is metastasized, that this cancer has grown from somewhere else and has now made it to his brain?"

And he responded, "That's exactly what I think."

I was stunned but oddly at peace and very clear about the path we had ahead of us. On the other hand, my mom and my aunt looked at him like he was speaking another language. They looked at me as if I was going to tell them he was joking. They were rocked to their core. My dad took it okay, but I knew he was terrified inside. They immediately put him on seizure meds, scheduled him for brain surgery three days later, and began doing other scans to see if there was cancer anywhere else. They found that he had stage four melanoma with tumors in his brain, lungs, spleen, pancreas, and liver. It was everywhere. My dad didn't know about any of this because he was in the middle of his first brain surgery.

Well, a little over a week later, after his second brain surgery due to a complication (long story), I was sitting in the ICU with both him and my mom. I had been spending the night there, making sure that he was okay, and then I would get up every morning and drive 30 minutes back to my house to get all my kids up, get them ready for school, get all their lunches set, and then drive them to the school near the hospital where I spent the day and the night. It was exhausting, but I felt like I just switched into a different gear, knowing what I had to do to take care of everyone. Thankfully, I have some great friends and an amazing wife who checked in on me and made sure I was doing okay. Anyway, that next morning, the oncologist came in. (Remember, my mom knew more about what was going on, but my dad had no idea what his diagnosis was a week and a half in.)

The doctor said, "Well, with stage four melanoma, there's just not a lot we could do, and with your history of autoimmune issues, there are not really a lot of options for us to help you with normal medicine." There was no, "Good morning, Mr. Haggerton. How's the breakfast?" He just said it like that and basically gave him a death sentence. My mom was sitting there, holding my dad's hand. I'm sitting in the room. My dad closes his eyes, lets his chin drop to his chest, and just starts to cry silently.

My dad's an old rancher who was born in the '50s when things were rough. I've rarely ever seen him cry. The only time I can remember was when his dad passed away while I was in the fourth grade. I saw tears start rolling down his face, so I firmly but respectfully pushed the oncologist out of the room. I thanked him profusely for his help, told him that we would get back with him as I maneuvered him out of the room, and closed the door behind him. I walked back over to the bed. I held my dad's other hand while he and my mom sat crying. We were quiet. I gave him what felt like an hour, but it was only a few minutes.

And then I just told him, "Dad, you get to feel whatever you need to feel at this moment. You get to be mad at God, mad at the doctors, and mad at the melanoma. If you want to be mad at that dermatologist that you think missed something, or if you want to be mad at the medication that you know lowered your immune system that allowed this to grow back, then do it. You can be mad at not getting to go fishing or whatever it is that you want to feel. You get to be depressed, you get to rage, you get to be scared." Then I told him, "But you only get 48 hours."

He looked up at me and asked through teary eyes, "Why 48 hours?"

I said, "Because in 48 hours, you need to make a decision, and we have to get to work because we have to figure out what we're going to do. We need to move ahead. We *have* to put action to this and get going because we choose to FIGHT. I'm gonna go take care of the kids. I love you, and I'll be back, but like I said, you get 48 hours."

He nodded, and I hugged my mom and left. In less than 24 hours, I returned to find my dad sitting up with a totally different look on his face. He looked at me and said, "I'm ready. Let's do whatever we need to do." He set his jaw, and with an intense look of determination, he said, "I'm not ready to die, and I've got a lot of things that I still need to do. I'm not done."

I have always known my dad was a strong man, but I had never seen the strength and resolve come out of him like I did that day. I'll never forget it. I was super proud of him. So I told him, "Okay, let's do it."

We did a lot of research, we made some decisions, and we went to a natural treatment center in Tijuana, Mexico, called Hope for Cancer. We gathered a team, and we moved ahead. And now, a year later, he is beating cancer. There's no more melanoma. He's fighting the other areas with more courage than most special forces soldiers and working every day to rebuild and strengthen his body. He's doing it.

He continues to fight this, stay on his protocols, and do what he's supposed to do. Are there repercussions from the brain surgery? Sure, are there little deficits in speech? Yes. Is his life totally different from what it was before having a baseball-sized tumor on the side of his head? Absolutely, but because he gave himself time to decide where he was at, he acknowledged the things that he felt, and then he made a decision not to quit. He's better, and he's doing good, and he's got years left in his life to do the things that the Lord's put on his heart. He can now pour into his grandkids and get time with the rest of his family.

The key to your story, just like his, is knowing where you are and not avoiding the feelings that you have so that you can truly feel them, get your brain wrapped around them, and actually make a decision. You can see them for what they are and make a decision, and be confident and at peace with that decision.

In life, there are always going to be seasons where you want to quit. In every single category of your life, you're going to have the opportunity to quit. You're going to have the opportunity to walk away, throwing a match into it all and burning the ships so you can do something totally different.

You're going to have the opportunity to quit on your marriage. At the end of our rope, when it was at the worst in our marriage, I wanted to quit. Cindy was stronger. For me, quitting would have been a lot easier than all the work that we had to do to get back to being healthy and in love.

What about finances? You will have opportunities involving your money where you think, *Man, I don't wanna do this anymore. This is too stressful, and I wanna quit.* When we were over $400,000 in debt, and we didn't think there was any way to get out of it, it would have been a lot easier to just quit. It would have been a lot easier to tap out and walk away and not do the hard work of admitting failure, rebudgeting, and selling things we loved, like our home and cars. It would have been easier to just quit, get regular jobs, and not push forward on the dreams that the Lord had put in our hearts. It would have been easier, but we didn't do it.

What about parenting? For those of you who are parents, it is a lot easier not to do the hard work and not to care. It's a lot easier not to do all the work you need to do with your little kids to build their character because it is exhausting. But kids are amazing. Parenthood is the best "hood" there is, but it is hard. It is the hardest, most thankless job on earth, and you're going to want to quit. They come into your life as cute little kids, and then they turn into teens. And as one of my closest friends says, they go from being a handful to being a "heartful." You go from dealing with little attitude problems to big heart problems while you're trying to grow them into amazing adults and humans, and not just regulate and corral choices and actions as little kids. If you haven't already, you will want to quit, walk away, and tap out. But if you do, you never get to see the other side. You never see them built into who they're created to be. And you miss out on the joy of the other side.

Look at any of your relationships, your friendships, and your business relationships. There are times you wanted to quit. When I was more immature, I had a real issue with walking away from people. I now know that all stemmed from me being adopted and having abandonment and rejection issues that I didn't even realize. But if I got into a relationship, whether it was a friendship, dating, or business, and that relationship got really hard, and the other person wasn't trying, and I was beating my head against the wall, I would do what I called light switch people, which today would be known as ghosting. I would just flip the light switch off. I could pull that lever, and they would no longer exist to me. I even told people in practice that my favorite word in the English language for people was "Next!" It wasn't healthy, but it was the way that I compensated. It was the way that I dealt with this feeling of rejection from people not doing the work to get better, at least how I thought they should. And so I would quit on them emotionally and mentally. It wrecked relationships and hurt the people I did it to.

Quitting is easy. It can be a cop-out. Sometimes, you gotta know when to quit, but quitting is a cop-out because it's just saying, "I don't wanna do the work." I get when it feels exhausting or overwhelming, and you'd rather hit the eject button than do it. You might want to just turn it off, like the old regular NES Nintendo. When we had friends over at my house, we'd play Nintendo all the time. We would be playing a game, and if they were losing really badly, they'd reach over and just hit the power button and turn it off, like, "Forget it, I'm done." Instead of finishing the game and losing, they turned the game off. Adults do that on a different level, hitting the reset button to make the pain stop and go away. Sometimes, the greatest lessons we'll ever learn, the deepest growth we'll ever experience, and the journey to becoming who we're meant to be all lie on the other side of pain. What if the person you're supposed to become is waiting there—and you don't push through?

What if all the development or who you're supposed to be as a husband and as a wife is on the other side of this pain? Maybe on the other side of this pain is the most beautiful marriage or the most beautiful relationship you could imagine. But you won't ever know if you don't push through the pain and the struggle.

If you don't push through the valley like we talked about in the last chapter, you never actually get to the mountaintop. What if this kid that you're struggling with, this teenager that you're having a hard time with, becomes an incredible adult after two years or three years of pain? If you don't wanna push through that, they won't become who they're supposed to be. We're better than that, and I know that you can do it. I know that you can get through that part, and you can push through the struggle to get to the other side. Pushing through what's uncomfortable and working through difficulty and working through all of that to get to the other side is called grit. It's actually one of the top factors that experts, like Angela Duckworth in her book *Grit*, have studied as the key difference between winners and losers—the difference between people who are consistently successful through failures and successes.

The thing that makes the difference in guys who are crushing it in life, like entrepreneurs and best-selling authors Gary Vaynerchuk and Grant Cardone, isn't that they're smarter than anybody else. It isn't that they were luckier than everybody else. It isn't that they had more favor than anybody else. It isn't any of those things. The number one factor that Duckworth studied in her book and that the experts have discovered is that the difference in people who succeed or not is number one, the choice to do it, and number two, grit. And grit is the measure of: Will you work hard when it gets hard? Will you dig in? Will you make the decision not to give up when things get really hard?

Now, we talk about not giving up when things get hard because it's the right thing to do or you're supposed to be there, like in your marriage or working hard, because you're supposed to be there. But what about when you should quit things?

What about the other side of quitting? How should you know when to quit certain things? Maybe you're in a bad relationship, and you know you should quit. I dated a girl in college, and I knew that I shouldn't be in that relationship. But I stayed in the relationship for too long because I didn't want to hurt her feelings. And I know a lot of people are this way. I've stayed in business relationships too long. I've stayed in situations with vendors, people that I've hired, or with employees. I've stayed in areas too long because of a fear of hurting people's feelings and letting people down instead of letting them go and allowing that relationship to end like I should have.

What about activities and things that you're doing? What if there's something in your life or things that you're doing or the things that you're into or things that you're addicted to, or things that you are involved in that you need to quit? Because part of you getting through the valley is you quitting those things because they're the very anchors or weights that are holding you back. You're not gonna get through that valley if there's something holding you back, like an addiction or a fear or a really bad relationship keeping you in that spot.

So, how do you know when to quit? Well, it goes back to Chapter 1's humility and being able to acknowledge your problems. This book is a revolving thing, and I want it to be more of a reference book for you to go back and forth into different chapters and come back to it in different seasons of your life. It's gonna be a book and a process attached to a community that you can use for the rest of your life at different points. When you think, *Oh man, Jim Bob said this in Chapter 7, but it referenced Chapter 1. I need to go back into the community and pull up the resources, the help, and the courses to get through this. I've got to keep looking at myself to know what activities and things I'm holding on to that I need to let go of.* Are there things and relationships that are in the way? It's just like cleaning out your closet every season.

When you're in a new season, you're like, *Oh, I need to go through my closet.* Cindy and I do this a lot. There are things in your closet that don't serve you anymore, that you shouldn't have anymore that you can give to someone else or give away or sell, right? It's the exact same way with the habits and relationships and things that you're doing in your life that aren't serving you and that aren't moving you forward. (Just don't give your bad habits to someone else. LOL.) Sometimes, you need to dig in and have grit to stay in areas so that you can get to the other side and succeed.

The other side of grit is knowing when to dig in and actually stop a thing. It's when you actually like to put your foot on the brake, shift that car back into park, and either get in a completely different car or change direction and go the other way. That takes grit. That takes as much grit, if not more, to stop a thing you shouldn't be in as to stay in a thing that you shouldn't. And it's understanding which one you need to do. In most situations, it's a little of both. It's a bit of understanding that we need to keep doing the things that we're called to and stop doing the things that we're not. That constant flow, that constant balance, and that constant tension throughout our lives are in each different scenario and season of our lives.

We should always ask the Lord, "What should I keep, and what should I let go or give up?" It's about walking into each scenario with open hands like, "Hey, Lord, what do you want to put into my hands? And what do you need to take out of my hands? And what do you need to put in and bless me with that I need to steward for you in this season? And what do I need to let go of? Because I don't need it if it's not serving me or my family anymore."

Choose what you need to do and choose what you need to stop. Make a list of it. Bring somebody in to actually give you feedback on this. If you don't know, then ask them if there are things you need to stop. Ask your spouse, ask your business partner, ask someone close to you, ask your pastor. One of the most beautiful things about being known by people in a community is you can ask them for feedback. I have so many people in my life who gladly tell me the things I need to stop doing, the things I'm not doing right, and the areas where I need to improve. As annoying and hard as it is, I'm so grateful for their honesty.

There are countless people who care about me enough to speak truth to me and say, "Bro, that thing you're doing, the way you talk to people over here, the way that you said that thing, how you handled that situation, you could have been better in that. You could have been more respectful. You could have been softer in that. You could have been more direct about that. You could have been less direct in that." And hopefully, I do that for them, too.

There was a book we used to recommend to parents to help them understand how to teach their kids about diet. Dr. Joanna Dolgoff wrote the *Red Light, Green Light, Eat Right* book, which had easy, simple visual analogies to show kids what foods were bad (red light), what foods were sometimes bad but not as horrible for you (yellow light), and what green light foods there were—the ones that they should always eat that are really good for them. I think that we could do this as adults and have red light, green light, and yellow light activities, relationships, and things in our life. Write down what are the green light relationships for you, the green light activities, and the green light goals for you? Write those down and move ahead on the things that are green light.

Make sure you have accountability in the things that are yellow light and just stop and move away from the things that are red light so that you can keep running this race that you're supposed to be. Ask yourself, *Why am I justifying the things that I'm doing, and why do I keep trying to do those things?*

"Not only so, but we also glory in our sufferings because we know that suffering produces perseverance; perseverance character; and character hope."

– (Romans 5:3-4)

These verses talk about grit but use the word perseverance. They talk about the journey we go through digging and doing the hard things. It also says how we have access to God through Jesus and access by faith into His grace. In verse three, it says we also can glory in the tribulations or things that are hard, knowing that tribulation produces perseverance (which is grit) and perseverance produces character (who we are and the choices we make when there's no one around), and character produces hope. Some of us have a problem with hope because we have a deficit of character.

We have a deficit of character because we refuse to do things that are hard to develop perseverance. Romans 5:5 says, *"And hope does not put us to shame, because God's love has been poured out into our hearts through the Holy Spirit, who has been given to us."* And so the thing that we need to get to that hope, to get to the window, to get to the doorway, or to get out of this dark room when we feel like there is no hope, is perseverance, doing the hard thing, and building grit to grow our character.

Once we build character, character produces hope.

Jersey Exchange

What jersey do you need to fix this? What jersey do we need to switch and exchange? You may have a jersey that you're putting on daily or wearing one that says QUITTER. And every day you wear that jersey you think, *I'm a quitter,* and you never finish things. You start things well, and you quit them when they get hard, or you never really fully try anything that's really impactful or has a purpose because you don't want to fail and you have a lot of fear. Maybe your jersey says FEARFUL.

Let's exchange that jersey from QUITTER for a jersey that says OVERCOMER. Or from a jersey that says FEARFUL to a jersey that says HOPEFUL or a jersey that says COURAGEOUS like we talked about in the last chapter. Lay that jersey down for quitter, and pick up the new jersey to move ahead.

Nerd Depot: The Science

After your brain has been stuck in a stress mode for so long, it begins to shut down to protect the vital organs and give you no options. It begins to give you no way out because it is trying to just focus on breathing in, breathing out, heartbeat, breathing in, breathing out, heartbeat. It does the normal things like digesting food, and it does the core things it needs to do on a daily basis just to survive because it knows that it can't do anything more because everything is just so tired. To get out of that mode, you have to do things to show the brain that there are more options. You have to start showing your brain what you need to do.

Action step: Journaling is one of my favorite techniques for helping you understand where you are and what you need to do to allow your brain to dump information out without burdening someone else around you and to develop a plan.

If you scan the QR code that follows, I've got training on journaling. I recommend doing journaling in what I call brain dump journaling, but also journaling to get a plan and go there, and I'll give you really good information.

But having a journal to be able to write things down, and even if you're just doing a basic gratitude journal for some time to remind your brain, these are the things that are going right. When everything feels like it's going wrong and you wanna quit, having a journal by the side of your bed to write down three things that you're grateful for and three things that you're hopeful for at the end of the day can be the difference in you staying the course and moving through that valley and getting to the other side and giving up. Being able to go back and read it is also helpful. Cindy read through my journals when our marriage was on the brink of divorce and it gave her so much hope that we could heal. It reminded her of who I really was and who I could be again.

Make sure you find a person or group that's gonna hold you accountable. Get them to help lead you through this valley. Reach out and ask for help. Sometimes the people around us can help us through the valley to the other side.

I want to get you a teaching I have on journaling and get you free access into a community that will help you move past your fears into ACTION and COURAGE!

SCAN THE QR CODE:

CHAPTER 8

Apathy

If you made it this far, first of all, I just want to congratulate you because getting through any book and finishing something is huge. Side note: If you are a person who has a problem with finishing things, I highly recommend Jon Acuff's book *Finish*.

In this section, I want to talk about something that really is basically the endpoint, the "end of the road" of not taking charge of all the things that you're dealing with, not taking charge of anxiety, not taking charge of understanding where you are, and not having grit. Whether by choice or you didn't even know there was another way or option, if you get to the end and feel like you've really hit a wall, that's where apathy resides. Apathy is beyond wanting to quit. It is completely checking out and where you disengage. I've been there, and I'm sure some of you have, too. It can happen to any of us.

Cindy and I have been blessed to mentor and work with so many couples (married and dating) since working through and healing in our own marriage. Some of the couples make it, but unfortunately some of the couples don't. But in the instances where the couples don't make it, it's because one of the spouses completely checks out, gets apathetic, and quits.

They literally disengage. They start disassociating in the relationship. And you can see this happen in other parts of your life too. Maybe you're in a job that you feel is a dead end, and you feel like there's nothing left you can do, or you're in a position where you are feeling like there's nothing more, and instead of pressing in and doing the best you possibly can in that scenario until there's another option, you completely check out. You completely do the minimum (or less) of what you're required to do in that situation just to get by, just to check a box.

There's no follow-through when you're apathetic. You don't follow through on relationships. You don't follow through on tasks you need to do. You don't follow through on basic things in your life to take care of the people around you. You don't follow through on things that are important to your kids. As your kids are hitting amazing milestones and they need you as a parent, you chose not to follow through and dropped the ball.

This is because you hit the point of apathy where you just don't care. It's the point where you feel like you're completely shutting down. Emotionally, you're completely shutting down. Mentally, at this point is when you start to abandon your principles, and truth and lies get blurry. You start to abandon things that would typically not even be a question or an option for you. Right before I began my affair in 2011, I had gotten to this point in my marriage with Cindy.

It happened quicker than I thought it could or would. We had become really disconnected, and we weren't talking. Our marriage had gotten really rocky earlier that year after the birth of our daughter, our second baby, and it got worse quickly. In the summer of 2011, I'll never forget, there was a point where I thought, *I don't care anymore, and I don't know why I'm trying.*

I didn't care anymore. I had convinced myself that Cindy was the problem. I had done everything I was supposed to as a husband (obviously a huge lie) and it was hopeless and pointless to try. That was the point I became vulnerable and made decisions that I would have never thought I was capable of making. So when temptation came in, and another option presented herself that never, ever, ever would have been an option for me before, I took it.

I took that next step and started creating another problem. This is how sin and mistakes work. You start with one, thinking the minute you say yes to this terrible thing that goes against your morals, everything will blow up around you. But these choices sometimes take months or years to show how devastating they really were, so you go further and further until you look back and don't even see the shoreline you started on.

Shortly after my first bad decision, I started drinking heavily every single night. I would go back to the townhouse I was living in, away from my family at the time. This was a second choice that never would have been an option for me before. I had hardly ever drunk alcohol. I was a doctor during all of this time with multiple office locations, multiple businesses, thousands of patients, respect in the community, a leader in our church, two beautiful kids, and an amazing wife. Everything was going well for me. But because I became apathetic, it opened the door for me to do things that I would have never actually considered and that I'd previously judged other people for doing up.

If you find yourself feeling apathetic, I'm just going to tell you I understand. I understand where you're at. I've been there. I understand what you're feeling. I understand that you're past the point of hopelessness, and you're at the point of wanting to throw a grenade into it all. You're past the point of just feeling overwhelmed, and you're at the point of wanting to hurt the people that are closest to you and wanting to hurt yourself. You're past the point of finding options, and you're ready to stop and give up. But I'm gonna tell you to wait. We went to a marriage intensive in the middle of our marriage hell over a weekend in Missouri. Our mentors told us not to make any decisions for six months to a year.

We had to do the hard work, try everything we could, get into counseling, do all the things that were in front of us, and pull every lever that was at our disposal for six to 12 months. And six to 12 months after that, if we had done all the work and things were working, and then there were no options, and we couldn't fix anything, we could choose to make other decisions at that point. And so it's the way we counsel couples now, and what I counsel business owners and parents with the situations that they get in. It works and keeps us from making rash decisions.

Seriously, do everything that you can do and do everything that you need to do before you do what you have to do. And do all the things that you're supposed to do. Do all the counseling, get somebody to come in and look at your finances, and do all those things before you completely shut down. One great quote that fits this I have seen circulate and on T-shirts says, "Pray like it all depends on God and work like it all depends on you." Do what you can, and let God do what He ultimately does. The biggest thing about shutting down is the mess that we leave on the way.

When we checked out—when I checked out of my marriage, checked out on Cindy, and walked away from her emotionally, mentally, and relationally—I left my mess behind. It's not like you clean up before you leave. It makes me think of when you go stay in a hotel room. I don't know about most of you guys. I don't do this, but I don't know how many of you guys make your bed and perfectly clean the hotel room before you leave. Uh, most of you don't. I would venture to say almost none of you do because that's not what you do when you are checking out of that hotel room. What happens when you're checking out is you leave all the towels on the floor, you leave your bed unmade, you leave your trash in a trash can, you probably even leave your key on the counter, and leave it because someone else, the cleaners, will come and deal with that mess.

Well, in life, we don't get to do that. In life, when we do that, we are leaving that mess for our spouse, our business partners, our boss, our investors, and our children. If we check out and walk away from the things that we are supposed to do and the things that we are responsible for or the things that we need to make a change on, it doesn't mean that everything's always going to work out perfectly. It doesn't mean that you know that marriage is going to work. It doesn't mean that the business can be saved in every single situation, but it means that because we have stepped into areas of responsibility and because we are adults in these different scenarios, we have a responsibility to see them through to the end.

We have a responsibility to stay on the deck of that ship until it fully goes under to make sure that everybody gets off. It's our responsibility to make sure that our kids are healthy, happy, and strong in any scenario, even if our marriage doesn't make it. It's our responsibility to see this ministry or nonprofit through to the end and to see these finances to where they need to be. It's our responsibility. We have to think of it that way. We have to step in as leaders and know that we are the ones who fall on it, and we have to walk it out. It takes extreme ownership.

Jocko Willink is a retired Navy SEAL, an amazing American hero, and now runs an executive coaching company called Echelon Front. He and his partner wrote a book called *Extreme Ownership,* which is one of the best leadership books I've ever read. In his book, he has a lot of anecdotes and stories about when he was in the Navy SEALs in Ramadi, running operations there. He talked about the key to leadership is taking extreme ownership of the outcome, which is the key to us being adults and leaders in any scenario.

Whether you're a parent of one child, a single parent, or working any job, you're a leader. True leadership means owning your role in everything—taking full responsibility for your actions and recognizing that the success or failure of any situation ultimately rests on your shoulders as the leader. We have to take responsibility for where we are to know that if we leave it, if we check out, and if we just let apathy take us over, we not only create a problem for the things that we're involved in, but it's gonna create a mess for everyone around us. It's gonna create a mess for anybody that comes behind us. It's gonna create a mess for any other group that follows us because we didn't take responsibility to do the things.

One of the hardest processes to go through to improve your marriage is you have to grieve what once was. Cindy and I had to mourn the marriage we thought we had in the middle of the affair. At the end of the affair, when we started healing, we had to go through a grieving process of our perfect marriage. We didn't have a perfect marriage. We had to acknowledge it, and we had to let what *was* die. We had to humble ourselves and realize that we were there because of my mistakes, bad communication and habits we had allowed to stay in our marriage, and mistakes and choices that I made after that. And that was something we had to work out. We had to allow that to be processed. We had to grieve and go through it.

The same thing happens in your business. When I shattered my femur, I had to shut down our chiropractic practice that we had built over 15 years. I had to close it all down because we couldn't keep it open without me in the office because I was in a wheelchair for a year. I had to grieve it and allow myself to feel part of our life was dying to be open to the next thing that the Lord had brought our way. But if we hadn't acknowledged it, that frustration could have led to apathy. I could have just laid there and stayed on pain meds and not moved ahead. I could have just never tried another thing and just stayed where we were. And we could have walked off and never reported to other people. We could have stopped encouraging people and stopped doing events. We could have stopped teaching. We were going to stop doing what we were called to do—stop walking out our calling, stop fulfilling what we were anointed to do—because of frustration, apathy, and anger over the things that happened.

Like the last chapter, always remember that there's another option and that when you start to feel that happens, you have to stop, back up, and ask for help. You have to pray and ask the Lord for peace and direction. Get really honest with yourself. Going back to the hotel room analogy, if I am traveling *with* someone, I've realized that I don't leave my hotel room nearly as much of a mess as if I'm traveling by myself. You know, it's that accountability piece that is so important. I keep all my stuff in one little area, and I clean it up to keep track of it. I leave the room better when I'm leaving it, even if I am checking out of an area, because of the people that are with me. Whether that's Cindy, a business partner, or one of my team members, having somebody on the journey with me holds me accountable to keep my mess in check, and to check out of things well, or to stay in an area that I should be in. And it's the same for me in every part of life, and it's the same for you. Who are you going along with on the journey?

I hope you see a pattern of this. I hope you see that in every single chapter, no matter what you're going through, part of the solution is the people you're around. Rob Wolf is a fantastic teacher and coach and has written amazing books on the Paleo diet. In one of his books, he talks about health and diet, but he also says that if one key factor is not in place and is not healthy, it doesn't matter what you do in your diet, you'll never be healthy. That factor is community. He says one of the most important factors in staying healthy and sticking to good habits is the people you surround yourself with. If you don't get community right, then you can do whatever you want with your diet, and whatever you want with your workouts, and you'll never get to full health because one of the main factors is people. I couldn't agree more, and my entire life is a testament to this fact.

It's more important than ever here in the apathy chapter, and I would actually go as far as to say that if you have the right people in your corner and on the journey with you, you will never get to this chapter. If you have the right people in your corner, they won't allow you to get to Chapter 8. I won't allow Cindy to get to this point because I want to push her to be all that she is created to be and all that she is put here on this earth to be for other people. She's a wife, a mom, a business leader, and an entrepreneur, and it is part of my duty as her husband to help push her into who she's meant to be.

Same with the people that I'm in business with and the same people that I partner with in coaching. It is my job and calling to push them into who they're supposed to be and not allow them to get to this point.

Apathy is beyond giving up. And unfortunately, in our society and American culture, one of the ultimate signs of giving up is suicide. There is an alarming growth rate of suicide among teenagers and among Gen Z in America that would shock you, break your heart, and terrify you all at the same time.

Over the past 20+ years, suicide rates among adolescent boys have increased by 137.8%, and among girls of the same age, the rate has risen by 179.3%.[1]

There is an organization called Stay Here, whose mission and entire goal through clothing lines and speaking is ministering to and educating these younger generations on the fact that they have hope and that suicide isn't their only option, but that part of hopelessness comes from isolation. We saw this grow to alarming rates during COVID and during lockdowns when people were isolated in their homes and isolated away from family and away from everybody else. We saw the instances of domestic abuse go through the roof, the instances of alcoholism, and the instances of suicide exponentially grow because when people are already stressed, already dealing with anxiety, already dealing with depression, and are then isolated, their apathy reaches a whole new level and people give up.

---

[1] Jennifer V. Verlenden et al., "Mental Health and Suicide Risk Among High School Students and Protective Factors — Youth Risk Behavior Survey, United States, 2023," *Morbidity and Mortality Weekly Report* Supplement 73, no. 4 (2024): 79–86, https://www.cdc.gov/mmwr/volumes/73/su/su7304a9.htm.

At the beginning of our mess, before I gave up on my marriage and before I became apathetic, we isolated as a couple. We left our small group as we were doing different things, and we isolated ourselves from every group that was really pouring into us. The only group we had was hanging out with the couple that I had the affair with. We pulled out of the community, blaming it on exhaustion and "busyness." You have to really pay attention and notice when you start to isolate and notice when people around you start to isolate.

A huge red flag should go off in your mind. This goes back to being known in your community. You have to pay attention to people around you in your inner circle and call them out when you see them start to isolate because once they start to do that, they're starting to get to the point of giving up. But you being here matters, you being in this situation matters, and you being in this marriage matters. People need you to be the best that you can be. They need you to be who you're called to be to help them be who they're called to be. They need you here. You're necessary in this marriage. You're necessary as a parent. You're necessary in this business. Even when you don't feel like it, you're necessary in this ministry. You're necessary in the story that you're in.

Jersey Exchange

What jersey do we need to exchange here? Well, you probably are wearing a jersey at this point of FINISHED or DONE or I DON'T CARE, and we need to change that jersey to BEGINNING, so I choose to get up and walk, or to keep walking. Let's change our jersey from

FINISHED to STARTING. Let's change our jersey from I'M DONE to I CHOOSE TO BEGIN. And let's walk ahead.

Nerd Depot: The Science

What happens in the brain? Well, it goes back to the fight-or-flight response that we continue to talk about, but the fight-or-flight response in this scenario is at the point where your hormone levels are at their all-time low, cortisol levels are at their all-time low, and you're probably already got into adrenal exhaustion because your body is designed to be able to wake you back up, to give you a jolt of energy so to speak, when it comes to the endocrine system and your hormones, to keep you going. When you feel like giving up, your entire neurology is designed to give you a breath and go, *Nope, we can do this.*

And that's where cortisol comes in and testosterone, DHEA, different hormones, norepinephrine, and epinephrine. They give you a jolt to keep you going in this boxing match called life. But when we've gone so far, and we've gotten so tired, or when we haven't slept well or eaten well, when we've treated our body like a theme park for so many years that now all those hormones are low and damaged and exhausted, then when you call on them, they can't respond. If they're a boxer, they literally can't hold their arms up, and when they're in that boxing match, they can't do anything for you, and that's where you start to see negative changes.

The QR code at the end of the chapter will take you to a course I did to help people with adrenal fatigue and shut down and give you exact tests, exact steps, and exact options on what you need to look at in order to get yourself out of having issues with adrenal fatigue and endocrine shutdown because if you're already at this point, it's really hard just to make a choice to get out of it.

The people around you matter, but your health matters more than ever at this point. If there is nothing left in the tank and your tank is empty, you can't start an engine. That's just common sense. If we're trying to start this amazing Ferrari, but there's no gasoline in the tank, you're not going anywhere. You're not improving, you're not able to work on that, and the longer that you stay out of gas, the longer you don't run that car, that amazing machine, the more things start to break down. Now the battery dies, all the cords and cables and hoses and pipes start to wear, and things start to break down in your body and your neurology. Your hormones are the same. And so there are things that you have to do and need to do to support your system with nutrition, supplements, and detoxes in order to help your body get to the point where it can handle the things you're in. The number one key is rest, reflection, and realization of where you are and that you matter. You are an integral character in the story that you're in. And without you, it's not the same. Knowing that and realizing that, you can start to take little steps to move forward to get more clarity and make better decisions.

Action steps: Find your purpose, get a coach or a mentor, or get a counselor. When things are so bad you really wanna disengage and don't care, it's time to get somebody to speak into the space. Get a mentor. It's important to partner with someone who is where you want to be and not struggling in the same pit you are in. It is vital for you to get a licensed counselor who can really speak to you and give you tips and referrals, or a coach who can challenge you and put words to the things you're struggling with and the things that you need or wanna do. They can help lead you through this fight into the next phase of your life and solutions so that where you are isn't where you stay.

I have an amazing course on adrenal health I want to gift you along with connecting you to a community that supports and loves you.

SCAN THE QR CODE:

CHAPTER 9

Bringing it All Together, Create Your Plan

YOU MADE IT! You're now at the end of the book's journey. However, you're gonna need to go through the process and evaluate what jersey you're wearing in different categories of your life over and over because the process of growing, improving, and pruning things out of our life and changing those jerseys is an ever-growing, ever-evolving process. The point of time when we stop evaluating if we need to change our jerseys is the point where we get off base and off track.

Looking back, what jersey did you have on when you started the book? And look at what jersey you're wearing now. What jerseys did you exchange? Did you exchange jerseys in the stuck portion? Was there a jersey that you needed to switch?

What jersey are you wearing now? Celebrate that! I mean, I think one of the things that's missing in our lives as adults, more than anything, is celebration. Think about it. As a kid, every time you do something little, even if it's dumb or if it's goofy, or if it's insignificant, we celebrate. Like you try to crawl, and you fall on your face, and we cheer like psychos because we think it's amazing. You eat an ice cream cone for the first time and drop it all over your face, but you do it yourself, and we cheer, and it's amazing.

At some point, as we age, we move into a phase where we no longer celebrate everything. Instead, we judge more, becoming overly critical of ourselves and those around us. Whether it's due to pressure, stress, competition, or expectations, we stop celebrating, cheering for ourselves, and supporting others. But we also want to celebrate you. And I'm over here slow clapping for you as you read this part of the book because I'm pumped. I'm pumped at any kind of progress that you make because, to be honest, finishing a book is a huge thing.

Finishing anything is a huge accomplishment. So well done looking at yourself. It's a hard thing to really take a humble look at yourself and dig deep to figure out the areas that you're proud of, but also the areas that could be better. The areas you know aren't doing well—and even the ones that could simply improve—are where change starts. Then comes the next step. As Tony Robbins says, "take massive action." Sometimes, it's that one decisive move that breaks you out of the rut and gets you moving in a new direction.

So, super awesome—you could've quit multiple times throughout this book, but you didn't. That's grit in action, exactly what we talked about in Chapters 7 and 8.

Getting through the book and not quitting translates into other areas of your life like your relationships, finances, and everything you do because every day you wake up and put your feet on the ground, you have a choice of what jersey to wear or take off. And so we have to be intentional every single day to look ourselves in the mirror and be honest about where we're at, how we're doing, how we can do better, and what we need to improve on.

At this point in the book, we want to develop a plan to help you move forward and help you improve in all of these areas and give you a plan to work through to come back to continue to work on these different areas of your life. It's easy to create another valley if you don't keep climbing. Remember, we talked about the valley, how we can get into a harder spot or in a low spot in our life, and that if we're not walking with the right people, we're not moving ahead. If we're moving in circles, we can get stuck, or if we sit down, we can get stuck in that valley. We can recreate another valley and come off of a mountain and make this other valley if we don't keep pushing, if we don't keep moving ahead, and if we don't keep our head up and we keep our eyes up and we pay attention to where we're at.

In life, in all of these different areas of your life, whether it's in relationships or business or finance or in leadership, if you're not growing or pushing, it means that you're dying. We're either getting better, or we're getting worse; there really isn't a plateau or a stagnant point. We can't just sit there and stay in one spot because, just like in health and fitness, we're either improving or our bodies are losing function. We're either getting healthier, or we're getting less healthy. We're not in a vacuum. We've got to consistently be passionate about accountability, be passionate about the people that are around us and in our corner, passionate about growth, and passionate about learning.

Mike Tyson says, "Everyone's got a plan until they get punched in the mouth." Know who's in your corner and press into them for accountability and growing and learning so that we never stay the same. If we are always focused on staying the same, or we're afraid to move to the next part because we're just afraid of it being hard or getting hurt again or failing, then we never experience who we are called and created to be.

Actually, if we stay the same, we're getting worse. And that's just a fact of it. I wanna encourage you in the area that you need to work on. Let's say it was anxiety, and you're holding back because of fear. If that's your area that you really need to work on, keep that in front of you. Keep it in the light, and keep it exposed to people around you so that you can move past it and put it behind you. But you can't just run by things you have to work on. That's what got you here in the first place and you're not that person anymore.

In order to move past it, in order to make sure that we are better people, you gotta keep it in front of you and keep it out ahead of you until you conquer it and move past it and grow beyond it. And then it can just be a mile marker on the journey of your life in the rearview mirror. So keep it in front of you so that people can help hold you accountable and can help you improve. No one reads a book like this and has problems in every single area of your life.

No one is dealing with all these things at once. No one is managing every category of their life perfectly at the same time. The truth is, most of us are thriving in a few areas, doing okay or struggling in one or two, and perhaps doing really poorly in another. There's always one main area that needs the most attention—it may even be affecting all the others. When I'm helping people with their health and wellness, and working through their symptoms, I often draw a chart I call the **Symptom Triangle**.

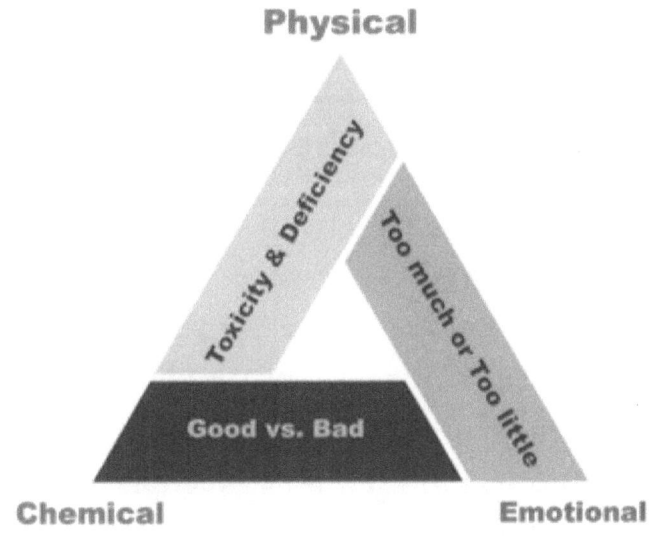

In the triangle, there are three different things that can cause symptoms, and you really can look at the different categories in this book as the exact same thing. So in the symptom triangle, there are three different types of stressors that can cause the body to not function well and create a symptom. These are either a physical stressor, an emotional stressor, or a chemical stressor, which is what you eat or what you put in or on your body. And then, within those categories, you're either getting too much bad or too little good.

This diagram really helps people to own and understand that what they need to focus on is different from someone else and they don't necessarily need to focus 100 percent in all three categories. Some people carry more emotional stress and trauma, which shows up in the bottom right-hand corner of that diagram. They need to work through that to help balance and reduce the symptoms they're experiencing. Others have a physical issue—like an injury—that needs to be addressed. They may be doing well in other areas, but the physical problem is what's holding them back. And for some, it's about making better lifestyle choices: cutting back on fast food, drinking more water, or taking high-quality supplements.

There are always categories that we need to work on. Remember, as you work on these different categories in your life that. You make sure you're not getting stuck in other ruts or falling into the "shame" trap. You're working on quieting the overwhelm that happens in your life. You're working on really just telling your brain what reality is versus lies and untruth. You're trying to keep from getting into depression. You're fighting that, you're battling the desire to want to quit, and you're trying to push through and build perseverance. And then, in the end, you're staying engaged and you're resisting apathy and making sure that you have grit.

When we are working on those things, there's not a time when we don't work on all of them; we just have to focus on some or more of the others. What I mean by that is, if we're really focusing on mindset, it doesn't mean that we don't focus on physical movement, eating right, communication, loving people around us, and pushing and developing grip. But sometimes we can get too focused—I feel like this is sometimes the trap that happens when people go to counseling and over-focus on one area. If they get help in one category, they think that everything needs to be focused on this one thing all the time, and they let everything else fall away.

This happens a lot with people dealing with tragedy in their marriage. We experienced this very thing when we were healing after my affair. As we finally got our heads above the water line and looked at other areas in our life, we realized our businesses and our finances had suffered because we were focusing so much on our marriage. I didn't do a good job of balancing all of them, and we had other problems to fix later. So just stay consistent and stay steady in the things that you need to work on because the rest of your life doesn't stop.

It takes awareness and evaluation to figure out what areas you can back off a little bit and come down in intensity. What areas do you need to not focus on? Or what areas do you need to completely let go of so that you can fully focus, heal, and grow in it so that you're a better person in that area?

Just be consistent; look at all these different areas and make sure that you are working really intentionally on the area that really spoke to you throughout this book, while also maintaining the other areas that are also important. One of the things that I would recommend you do is look at the different chapters, and when you know which chapter really speaks to you (there may be more than one), you're gonna pour into that chapter, do the practical things, look at the QR codes, watch the videos, get into the community that we've built for you here, and talk to other people that are on the same journey as you.

I recommend devoting three months to be able to work on that one category. Actively work on understanding:

1. Why were you wearing that jersey in the first place?
2. Finding a healthy replacement for that jersey through the active steps that we are giving you in this next section.
3. Getting the right support to help you walk it out.

This is gonna really help you own that one area, and you're not gonna rush through the different steps. The actions, the habits, and the process of walking this out are more important than the goal at the end. It's even more important than what happens when you get through it. One of the best books focusing on the process of more than the goal is called *Atomic Habits* by James Clear. It is one of the best books on goal setting and attaining our goals out there on the market. In the book, Clear talks about how people set goals. And as you read a book like this, it's really easy to set a goal.

It's like setting the goal to reset your mindset. But you set a goal without setting proper habits and systems and processes along the way. You reach this goal early on or quickly without the foundation of the habits that are needed to keep that goal going. Once we hit the goal, we just abandoned it because there was no substance and no foundation to continue it. So we have to do tiny actions and changes, set up systems and set up things to make sure that after we work on our mindset, or after we work on developing grit and being consistent, that we get to our goal and we stay there. We don't want to get to our goal and lose it and have to reset the goal all the time; it's no different from yo-yo-ing back and forth on weight loss and weight gain. We don't want to do that. We don't want to be those people. We want to hit our goal, stay there, be healthier in our marriage, be healthier in our bodies, be healthier in our finances, and continue to move and improve from that point on.

In order to move through this, the first thing you're really going to have to do is identify your why and your purpose for doing it. If you're just doing it because someone told you or because Jim Bob wrote it in Chapter 7, it's never gonna be a long-term change for you because you did it for someone else, or you did it because someone else suggested it.

There's gotta be a purpose greater than you and a purpose to do it where you're pouring into yourself because of someone else or because of this greater reason to keep you going on this path. So, really think through it. Get a journal and ask yourself, why do I need to change? Why do I wanna be better? Why do I wanna wear a new jersey in this category? And what is in it for those around me? How is this gonna make my life, my sphere, and the people around me in my community better? See the faces of your family, your kids, and your co-workers in this step. Make it personal.

It takes 120 days to really achieve cellular change when you're changing habits. Research done by Dr. Caroline Leaf, best-selling author of *Switch on Your Brain*, looked at how long it takes to create neuroplasticity change in the brain. This basically means the activity it takes to make the nerves do something different. If the nerve is used to doing A, you have to retrain it and tell it something completely different to have it do B in a completely different action. What they found is that it takes a minimum of sixty-two days to start to form a long-term habit. To create cellular change and a lifelong habit, we want you to take these steps and take our 12-week, 120-day challenge and plan.

If you scan the QR code below, it will lead you to a page where you can start building your plan out, deciding what area you need to work on, and the steps it's gonna take to get to that next level.

That 12-week goal can be broken down into weekly accountability goals and weekly actions and tactical things that you need to do, say, think, or feel on a daily basis to be able to not only put you in the right direction but get you to the right destination and keep you there long-term. It's more about the journey and where you're going, getting there, staying there, and continuing to move in that direction, then setting a goal and getting excited and sitting down in the goal because the goal itself can become a valley if we stay there.

We don't wanna stay in a place, even if it's amazing, any more than we wanna stay in a place that's not amazing or that is bad because we wanna constantly be improving, which, again, goes back to the growth mindset.

So, go to this link below, pick the category that you know that you really felt called to work on, set up your plan, start your actions, set up your habits, and then let's get you on another path to a new destination, and in 12 weeks you won't even recognize who you were.

Remember, we don't grow by knowing; we grow by DOING.

Scan this QR code for a free 12-week action plan to get you started!

SCAN THE QR CODE:

Conclusion

Well, you did it.

There are so many things that we covered in this book, and there's so much information and so many stories that sometimes it can feel overwhelming, which is why I wanted to create each chapter as its own guide and plan and create QR codes with teaching and videos attached to each one. So, make sure you click on each of those. But if you read through the book, there are a couple of main things that really stand out that are important that I want you to walk away with.

Number one: it's okay to feel the way you feel. It's okay to be where you are. It's just not okay to stay there. Just remember that it is 100 percent okay, and it's not your fault in many situations, and it's not that you're broken or wrong or something's wrong with you and where you are, but acknowledging where you are means that we have to choose to go somewhere different.

Number two is your community matters. People that are around you are either going to push you forward or hold you back. They're either going to push you into who you are called to be, or they're going to pull you into who they want you to be to make them feel better about themselves. So, be intentional with your community.

Number three: get a plan and start, and let us help you. We want to guide you along the way. We want to hold your hand along the process. We want to stand right beside you and right behind you so that if (or when) you stub your toe along the way, we can help catch you and redirect you. We can high-five you at the end, and along the way, as you're doing amazing things, and we can celebrate you along this journey of getting better in every area of your life.

I know you can do this. I know that if you pick a plan and you make a choice to do better in any area of your life, and you keep putting one foot in front of the other, the only logical possibility is that you're going to be in a new place soon. I know because I have done it myself.

You're going to turn around in a month and be in a different place than you are today. You're going to turn around in six months and be in a completely different place than you are today. You're going to turn around in 12 months, 18 months, two years, five, ten years down the road, and you're not even gonna recognize where you were when you started this process, but all it takes is the first step. And I know you can do it, and we wanna help you.

Thank you. Thank you for going on this journey with me. Thank you for trusting me with your time. Thank you for being vulnerable and being humble enough to admit that there are things that you want to improve on. Thank you for doing the work. It makes all of this worth it. It makes all of our stories as a family, and the things that we've walked out have a purpose, knowing that you've gotten through this book and have been able to use the things that we have walked through and the experiences that we've had.

I hope that throughout this book, you've realized that community and connecting with other people who are on the same journey as you are so vitally important. So we want you to join us. Scan the QR code below to stay in contact with us. Please join the community. Jump in there and help us make this community the most solid community that there is in the realm of personal development and improvement. Share with your friends. Friends don't let friends stay where they're at, and friends don't let friends not grow personally, so share it. Let's all get better together.

You can do it. We can help. Be well.

QR Code: Link to the community

Custom Jerseys: Link to our site to create their own custom jerseys

THANK YOU FOR READING MY BOOK!

DOWNLOAD YOUR FREE GIFTS

Just to say thanks for buying and reading my book, I would like to give you a few free bonus gifts, no strings attached!

Scan the QR Code:

I appreciate your interest in my book and value your feedback as it helps me improve future versions of this book. I would appreciate it if you could leave your invaluable review on Amazon.com with your feedback. Thank you!

www.ingramcontent.com/pod-product-compliance
Lightning Source LLC
Chambersburg PA
CBHW030247010526
44107CB00031B/1348/J